Contents

Introduction ii
Tracking Progress Chart iii

Reading Test Tips and Practice
Standardized Tests for Reading 2
Test Tips for Reading Literature 4
Literature Selections 9
Test Tips for Reading Informational Texts 20
Informational Text 24

Language Arts and Vocabulary Test Tips and Practice
Standardized Tests for Language Arts 33
Test Tips for Grammar and Usage 33
Test Tips for Mechanics 36
Language Arts Practice 39
Standardized Tests for Vocabulary 47
Test Tips for Vocabulary 47
Vocabulary Practice 51

Writing Test Tips and Practice
Standardized Tests for Writing 56
Scoring the Writing Prompts 56
Test Tips for Responding to a Prompt 59
Graphic Organizers for Writing 60
Writing Prompt 1: Opinion 64
Writing Prompt 2: Informative 72
Writing Prompt 3: Narrative 80

Practice Tests
Reading Practice Test 89
Language Arts Practice Test 109
Vocabulary Practice Test 117
Writing Practice Test 122

Answers
Answer Sheets 131
Answer Key 135

Introduction

This book is a tool to give your students practice in taking standardized tests. Research shows that students who are acquainted with the scoring format of standardized tests score higher on those tests. The concepts presented in this book are typically found on standardized tests in Reading and Language Arts for this grade level. The goal of this book is to improve students' ability to perform well on standardized tests. Students will have multiple opportunities to practice answering items in multiple-choice format, as well as to respond to open-ended items and writing prompts.

The tracking progress chart can help you pinpoint areas of weakness and strength with particular skills.

The book is divided into two main sections. The first section includes Test Tips and Practice for four main areas: Reading, Language Arts, Vocabulary, and Writing. Each Test Tips section provides a review of common skills and terms as well as strategies related to the topic. The Reading section focuses on literary texts (stories, poems, and drama) and informational texts (nonfiction and technical). The Language Arts section covers grammar, usage, and mechanics, as well as editing and revising skills. The Vocabulary section covers skills related to vocabulary acquisition, such as using context clues to determine the meaning of unfamiliar words and analyzing word relationships. The Writing section focuses on three types of writing prompts: opinion, informative, and narrative.

The second section provides Practice Tests for each area. For an authentic testing experience, students will record their answers to test items on an answer sheet.

Tracking Progress Chart

Objective	Practice Item	Test Item	Mastery Yes	Mastery No	Comments
Literary Texts					
Understand and analyze plot.* (RL.5.2)	**8, 16**	**8**			
Understand and analyze characters.* (RL.5.2)	**1**	**17**			
Understand and analyze setting.	**14**	**2, 12**			
Understand and analyze theme.* (RL.5.2)	**6, 23**	**7, 14**			
Understand and analyze point of view.* (RL.5.6)	**4, 10**	**4, 19, 26**			
Understand and analyze elements of poetry.	**25**	**18**			
Understand and analyze literary devices.	**20, 24, 27**	**16, 21**			
Understand and analyze elements of drama.	**13**	**11**			
Make inferences from literary text.* (RL.5.1)	**11, 15, 18, 28**	**5, 15, 24**			
Analyze and understand elements and structures of literary texts.	**3**				
Understand and analyze figurative language, such as similes and metaphors.* (RL.5.4)	**5, 29, 30**	**1, 23, 25**			
Identify specific details and events in a literary text.	**9, 12**	**13**			
Compare and contrast characters, settings, or events in a literary text.* (RL.5.3)	**2, 19, 22**	**9**			
Analyze how illustrations contribute to the meaning of a literary text.* (RL.5.7)	**26**	**6, 22**			
Identify and understand connotative use of language in literary texts.	**17, 21**	**10, 20**			
Summarize literary texts.* (RL.5.2)	**7**	**3**			

*Aligns with Common Core State Standard

Objective	Practice Item	Test Item	Mastery Yes	Mastery No	Comments
Informational Texts					
Identify the main idea of a text and the details that support it.* (RI.5.2)	7, 14	6, 12			
Analyze an author's perspective, argument, and point of view.	9	2			
Analyze how text structures of informational texts contribute to the development of ideas.* (RI.5.5)	12, 19, 24	7, 10			
Make generalizations from a text.	6				
Make inferences from an informational text.* (RI.5.1)	1, 16, 20, 23	13, 15, 18			
Analyze and understand elements and features of informational texts.	11, 15, 21	11			
Summarize informational texts.	26				
Identify specific details, facts, or events in a text.* (RI.5.1)	4, 5, 8, 17, 18, 22	1, 5, 9, 16			
Analyze how media and graphics contribute to a topic or issue.	25	3			
Identify and understand academic, domain-specific, and technical words in informational texts.* (RI.5.4)	3, 13	4, 17			
Evaluate arguments and claims and how they are supported by evidence.* (RI.5.8)	2, 10	8, 14			

Objective	Practice Item	Test Item	Mastery Yes	Mastery No	Comments
Language Conventions					
Demonstrate control of grammar, usage, and sentence structure.* (L.5.1)	9, 16, 17	10, 19			
Use complete sentences and recognize and correct fragments and run-ons.	8	1			
Correct inappropriate shifts in verb tense.* (L.5.1)	1, 14	2, 7			
Use correlative conjunctives correctly.* (L.5.1)	6, 12	3, 13, 14			
Use precise words and phrases to convey ideas.	7	20			
Understand agreement.	11	4			
Use verbs correctly, including perfect tenses.* (L.5.1)	2, 13	11, 12			
Use pronouns correctly.	3, 15	15			
Combine sentences and vary sentence patterns for meaning, interest, and style.* (L.5.3)	18, 19, 20	16, 17, 18			
Use adjectives and adverbs correctly.	4	5, 8			
Use frequently confused words correctly.	5	9			
Avoid common usage problems.	10	6			
Demonstrate control of standard English conventions and mechanics.* (L.5.2)	27, 34, 38	21, 36, 39			
Use capitalization correctly.	22, 40	29			
Use punctuation correctly.* (L.5.2)	25, 26, 28, 36	24, 26, 30			
Use commas correctly (introductory clauses, interjections, and direct address).* (L.5.2)	24, 32, 35	22, 27, 32, 35			
Use underline, quotation marks, or italics for titles of works.* (L.5.2)	31, 33	33, 37			
Use quotation marks correctly.	21, 37	23, 31			
Use correct spelling.* (L.5.2)	23, 29, 30, 39	25, 28, 34, 38			

Objective	Practice Item	Test Item	Mastery Yes	Mastery No	Comments
Vocabulary					
Understand common idioms, adages, and proverbs.* (L.5.5)	9	4			
Identify synonyms and antonyms.* (L.5.5)	3, 10, 11	3			
Use context clues in words, sentences, and paragraphs to decode new vocabulary.* (L.5.4)	2, 7	5			
Identify and understand connotative and figurative use of language.* (L.5.5)	12	1			
Identify and use correctly multiple-meaning words.* (L.5.4)	1, 13	8, 10			
Understand academic and specialized vocabulary.* (L.5.6)	4	2, 11			
Identify and use suffixes, prefixes, and roots to understand and create words.* (L.5.4)	6	12			
Interpret figures of speech, such as simple similes and metaphors.* (L.5.5)	5	9			
Understand word relationships.* (L.5.5)	14, 15	7			
Understand how to use dictionary entries to determine pronunciation and clarify meaning.* (L.5.4)	8	6			
Writing					
Write opinion essays.* (W.5.1)	Prompt 1	Prompt 1			
Write informative essays.* (W.5.2)	Prompt 2	Prompt 2			
Write narrative essays.* (W.5.3)	Prompt 3	Prompt 3			

Tracking Progress Chart
Higher Scores on Reading and Language Arts, Grade 5

Reading Test Tips
and Practice

Standardized Tests for Reading

In the Reading Practice section, you will read some general strategies for answering multiple-choice questions and open-ended questions. Then, you will review common literary terms, comprehension skills, and reading skills related to literary and informational texts. After you review the terms and skills, you will read literary and informational selections and answer questions about them.

Strategies for Answering Multiple-Choice Questions

Here are some suggestions for taking a reading test:

- **Read the passage as though you were not even taking a test.** Get a general understanding of the topic and purpose of a passage. You may not understand everything at first, but keep reading.

- **Look at the big picture.** As you read, look for the main features of the selection. Ask yourself the following questions as you read:

  - What is the title?

  - For a literary selection, such as a story, play, or poem, what is the theme or main message? For a nonfiction selection, what is the main idea?

  - What is the author's purpose for writing the selection? Is the purpose to inform, entertain, persuade, or show how to do something?

- **Next, read the questions.** This will help you know what information to look for when you reread.

- **Reread the passage.** Underline information that relates to the questions. Jot down your notes or questions in the margin as you read. You can use them to help you answer the questions.

- **Go back to the questions.** Try to answer each one in your mind before looking at the answer choices. Circle any important words in the question. This can help you understand what the question is asking.

- **Finally, read *all* the answer choices.** Cross out any answer choices that you know are incorrect. Then, choose the best answer. You may need to go back to the selection and look for information. Pay attention to what the question asks. For example, if it asks for a main idea, look for a choice that is a broad concept, not a narrow detail.

Strategies for Answering Open-Ended Questions

Some standard reading tests include open-ended questions. These questions do not have answers for you to choose from. Instead, you must write a response to the question. Open-ended questions can require a short answer or an extended response of multiple paragraphs. Most open-ended questions test your ability to use what you have learned from reading a selection. Here are some suggestions for answering open-ended questions:

- Read the entire selection. Pay attention to important information, such as major events and characters or main ideas and details. Jot down information you believe is important about the selection.

- Read each question carefully.

- Think about what the question is asking before you answer it. There are some words that appear frequently in open-ended questions, such as *compare*, *contrast*, *explain*, *interpret*, *describe*, and *summarize*.

- Return to the selection and skim it. Look for the details or examples that will support your answer.

- When writing your answer, be precise but brief. Refer to details from the selection. Be sure to proofread for spelling, grammar, and punctuation errors.

- If you cannot answer the question at first, skip it and return to it later.

How Open-Ended Reading Questions Are Scored

Open-ended questions are scored based on how well they meet certain criteria. Here is an example of how open-ended questions might be scored:

Score of 3: This response has a correct answer. It is supported by information from the selection. It also has specific, appropriate, and accurate details or examples.

Score of 2: This response has only a partial answer. It shows awareness of what is to be answered, and has at least one detail from the selection. Although this response attempts to provide sufficient examples, it may contain minor inaccuracies.

Score of 1: This response is incomplete. Either the question was misunderstood, or no details from the selection were included in the response. The examples are insufficient or inappropriate, and there may be major inaccuracies.

Score of 0 This response has too little information to be scored or is inaccurate in many ways. The following conditions will cause a response to receive a score of 0:

- The response is blank or too short to be scored.

- The response is off-topic.

- The response is written in a language other than English.

- The handwriting in the response is unreadable.

Test Tips for Reading Literature

Reading tests contain different types of literary selections. Literary selections can include fiction, plays, and poems. Knowing the features of different literary selections can help you understand them and answer questions about them. Here are descriptions of different types of literature:

Fiction

Fiction tells a story about made-up rather than real events. There are many types of fiction. For example, a **myth** is a type of story that usually describes a hero or famous event. Myths often explain how something came about. A **fable** is a story that teaches a lesson. Fables usually have animal characters. A **folktale** is a traditional story or legend that has been passed down orally for many generations. A **fictional diary** or **journal** tells the events in a made-up person's life. **Historical fiction** tells about a real person or event in history. Although the characters and some events might have been real, historical fiction is meant to tell a story and not simply give information about the past.

Drama

A drama is a play. It is a piece of literary writing meant to be performed by actors. Most plays begin with a **cast of characters**. This is a list of the different parts in the play. When you read a play, you'll see that the name of the character comes before the words the character says. Many plays also have **stage directions**. They explain what the characters are doing, where they are, and how they are saying their lines. Usually, the stage directions are in italic type, inside parentheses, to show that they are not meant to be spoken aloud.

Poetry

A poem expresses feelings and ideas or tells stories using rhythm and imagery. The author of a poem is called a **poet**. The narrator of a poem is called a **speaker**. Poetry is written in **lines**, which are the words in one row of the poem. A line of poetry is not always a complete sentence. A **stanza** in poetry is a group of lines, similar to a paragraph. A **rhyming poem** includes words that rhyme. The rhyme usually follows a pattern; for example, the same lines in each stanza will end with rhyming words. **Free verse poetry** does not have rhyming words. Lines in free verse poems may vary in length and not follow a pattern of beats.

Summarizing

Follow these steps to choose the best answer to a **summary** question:

Step 1: Look for the main characters, conflict, and the most important details, such as actions and events, as you read the passage slowly and carefully.

Step 2: Consider every answer choice. Get rid of those that restate a single detail from the passage, make a general statement about the passage but include no important details, or have little or nothing to do with the passage.

Step 3: Be sure that the answer you choose covers the *entire* passage. It should include the main conflict, characters, and major supporting details.

Making Inferences

You make an **inference** when you use what you've read in a passage and what you already know to determine something the author hasn't stated directly. Use the following steps to answer inference questions:

Step 1: Read the passage carefully.

Step 2: Locate key words and phrases in the answer choices that match similar words and phrases in the reading passage. You may be able to get rid of some answers right away.

Step 3: Confirm your answer by considering your prior knowledge about the subject of the passage.

Drawing Conclusions

You may be asked questions that begin like this: "Why do you think . . ." or "Based on the information in the selection . . ." Questions like these require you to draw a **conclusion**. Use the steps below to respond to these types of questions:

Step 1: Read the question to identify the topic.

Step 2: Study the answer choices, ruling out those choices that are clearly wrong.

Step 3: Reread the selection and look for evidence that supports one of the remaining answer choices.

Analyzing Characters

A **character** is a person or animal in a story, play, or other literary work. A writer can develop a character in several different ways:

- by describing how the character looks and dresses

- by telling the reader what the character says

- by showing the reader how the character acts

- by letting the reader know the character's thoughts and feelings

- by revealing what other characters think or say about the character

- by telling the reader directly what the character is like (kind, cruel, or brave, and so on)

Identifying Setting

Setting is the time and place of a story, play, or poem. The setting can help create a mood, help you understand the story's problem, or affect the events of the plot.

Analyzing Plot

Plot is the series of events that makes up a story. Many plots have the following structure:

- An **introduction** tells who the characters are and what their **conflict**, or problem, is.

- **Complications** arise as the characters take steps to resolve the conflict.

- The plot reaches the **climax** at the most exciting moment in the story.

- The final part of the story is the **resolution**. This is when the characters' problems are solved and the story ends.

  When analyzing a story or play, you can look for the story's **problem** and **solution**. Look for what happens in the selection. How do characters try to fix the problem?

Identifying Point of View

Point of view refers to who is telling a story. Two common points of view are **first person** and **third person.**

- In first-person point of view, one of the characters, using the pronoun *I*, tells the story. The reader can know only what the narrator knows or observes.

- In third-person point of view, the narrator knows everything about the characters and events in a story. Sometimes, a third-person narrator tells the story through the point of view of one of the characters. The reader will know only what that character thinks and feels.

Analyzing Theme

The **theme** of a story is the main message, lesson, or truth about life that the author is trying to express. A theme is not usually stated directly in the work. You will have to make an inference about a work's theme based on characters and events. Follow these steps:

Step 1: Think about the main problem in the story and how the characters react to it.

Step 2: Ask yourself if the characters learned any lesson about life or made any discoveries about themselves, others, or the world around them.

Step 3: Choose the answer that describes the overall message of the selection.

Analyzing Tone

An author's **tone** is how he or she sees the world or events in a literary work. Authors create a tone through their choice of words and examples. For example, the author might include examples of scary situations to create a tone of suspense. Use the following steps to answer questions about a writer's tone:

Step 1: Look at the writer's choice of words and examples. What do they tell you about the writer's attitude toward the subject?

Step 2: Read all the answer choices. Get rid of answer choices that are not supported by the author's word choices and examples.

Step 3: Reread the remaining answer choices. Choose the one that best describes the tone of the passage.

Identifying Literary Devices

Literary devices are techniques writers use to help you imagine the topic. Here are some common literary devices you might see in reading test selections:

Alliteration—repetition of the same or very similar consonant sounds in words that are close together.

> **Example:** The wind whispered sweet sounds.

Connotative language—language that creates a certain image or feeling in a reader's mind. Writers make certain word choices to influence the meaning of a text.

> **Examples:** Tom had a big, empty room. Tom had a spacious, airy room.

Figurative language—describes one thing in terms of another and is not meant to be taken literally.
A **metaphor** compares one thing to something quite unlike it.

> **Example:** Meg was a tank pushing her way to the front of the line.

A **simile** compares two unlike things using *like* or *as*.

> **Example:** His voice was like a mosquito whining in my ear.

Personification gives human qualities to an object, plant, or animal.

> **Example:** The dog smiled and winked knowingly at me.

Imagery—language that creates a picture in the mind using any of the five senses: sight, touch, smell, hearing, and taste.

> **Example:** As we sat around the fire, the wood crackled and popped as the flames danced and warmed us with a gentle touch.

Rhyme—repetition of accented vowel sounds and all sounds following them.

> **Examples:** greet, sweet; humble, grumble

Literature

In this selection, a traveler teaches some villagers a valuable lesson. Read the selection. Then, answer the questions. On your answer sheet, darken the circle for each correct answer for multiple-choice items. For the short-answer item, write your answer on a separate sheet of paper.

Stone Soup: A Swedish Folktale

There once was a man who had been traveling for many years. He was exhausted and hungry, so he decided to stop in a village to rest and eat. When the villagers saw him, they hurried to put away their food. They did not want to share what they had with strangers.

The traveler decided to teach them a valuable lesson. He went to the middle of the village square, put down his pack, and took out a shiny black soup pot, a big spoon, and a sharp knife. He filled the pot with water, built a fire, and set the pot on the fire. Soon the water in the pot began to bubble. The villagers peeked curiously out of their windows as they watched the traveler pick up a handful of small stones and drop them carefully into the steaming water. Then, he stirred and stirred the pot.

One of the village women walked over to the traveler, asking, "What are you making in that pot, sir?"

"I'm making stone soup," the traveler replied. "It is almost done, and it's very delicious! Now if I only had one carrot, the flavor would be just perfect."

"I have one carrot," the woman said, and she ran home to get it. The traveler cut the carrot into pieces and added it to the pot.

In a few minutes, a man came out of his cottage to see what was happening. "What's in the pot?" he asked the traveler.

"I am making stone soup," the traveler explained. "It is almost ready, but if I only had one onion, how much better my soup would be!"

"I have one onion," said the man, and

he went back to his house, returning with a large yellow onion. The traveler cut the onion into slices and dropped the slices into the bubbling pot.

Soon a small circle of curious observers had gathered around the traveler and his pot of stone soup. Occasionally, the traveler would remember another thing that would add more flavor to his soup. For example, he would say, "If only I had some potatoes!" Almost immediately, someone would run home to fetch some. Then, he would say, "If only I had some tasty green beans," and as fast as lightning, someone would get him some. Then, he said, "A few beets and peas would really improve my soup."

Presto! Beets and peas would appear and be added to the pot. The pot continued to fill up with many ingredients. Finally, the traveler said, "If only I had some salt and spices!" Many villagers scurried home to fetch salt, pepper, thyme, and other herbs and spices.

Soon everyone in the village had gathered in the square to watch the strange traveler stir his soup. A delicious smell wafted through the air. "It's done!" the traveler cried happily. He filled a mug with the steaming liquid and then offered the rest of the soup to the villagers. Each one enjoyed the soup, and each one thought it was a miracle that soup made out of stones could taste so good.

1. From his words and actions, what can you tell about the traveler?

   A He is silly.

   B He is angry.

   C He is clever.

   D He is lazy.

2. At the beginning of the selection, how are the villagers different from the traveler?

   A They are shy.

   B They are friendly.

   C They are hungry.

   D They are selfish.

3. Which sentence is true of folktales like "Stone Soup"?

   A They are passed down through generations.

   B They are fiction stories about real people.

   C They have made-up people but real events.

   D They tell about a hero or famous event from history.

4. At the end of the selection, why do the characters think the soup is a miracle?

   A They have never tasted soup before.

   B They do not realize all the things they added to the pot.

   C They never saw someone cook such a large amount of soup.

   D They do not know where all of the ingredients came from.

5. Read this sentence from the selection.

   > Then, he would say, "If only I had some tasty green beans," and as fast as lightning, someone would get him some.

   Why does the author refer to lightning?

   A to show how quickly something happened

   B to describe what the weather was like

   C to explain the loud sound of thunder

   D to tell about a bright flash of light

6. What is the theme of the selection?

   A People must be careful about what they share with strangers.

   B If you want to do something the right way, do it yourself.

   C If each person gives just a little, together people can do a lot.

   D It is more enjoyable to give than it is to receive.

7. Summarize the selection.

Name _____   Date _____

In this selection, a boy prepares a project for a science fair. Read the selection. Then, answer the questions. On your answer sheet, darken the circle for each correct answer for multiple-choice items. For the short-answer item, write your answer on a separate sheet of paper.

The Science Fair

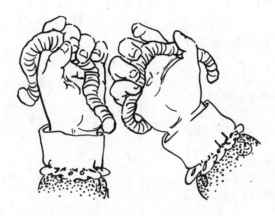

Rick was very proud of the project he had entered in the science fair. He had built a worm house. He intended to show how long it takes worms to eat different types of kitchen scraps. Rick's hypothesis, the idea that he was trying to prove, was that worms eat and process some foods faster than others. He was so proud of his project that he constantly bragged to his friends about it. After a few days, Rick's friends were tired of hearing about Rick's worm house.

Finally, the day of the fair arrived. First, Rick set up the display board behind the worm house. Every time he let go of the board, however, it started to fall. Rick was alarmed. People would not understand his hypothesis if they couldn't read the display board. Rick

tried once more to stand up the display board. For a moment, he thought it was going to stay, but then it crashed down. Worst of all, it knocked the worm house onto the floor! Now wiggly worms and scraps of old food were everywhere. Rick's project was ruined, and there was no chance of winning the science fair.

At first, Rick was upset, especially when his friends laughed at the mess. Rick felt a little better when they offered to help him clean it all up. He even laughed when his friends offered a suggestion: "Now you can make a hypothesis about how long it will take us to clean up this mess!"

8. Which of these events happened first?

   A Rick bragged about his project.

   B Rick built a worm house.

   C Rick's friends laughed at the mess.

   D Rick's project was ruined.

9. How did Rick's friends react at the end of the selection?

   A They offered to help Rick clean up.

   B They turned the display board around.

   C They quickly left the science fair.

   D They pretended they didn't know Rick.

10. Why does the author describe how Rick's friends feel about his bragging?

    A to show that Rick's friends dislike the project

    B to show that Rick's friends are losing patience with Rick's behavior

    C to show that Rick's friends hope someone else will win the science fair

    D to show that Rick's friends are tired of feeding food scraps to the worms

11. How does Rick most likely feel on the morning before the fair?

    A embarrassed

    B nervous

    C concerned

    D excited

12. Give two reasons why the science fair didn't go as planned for Rick.

Name _____   Date _____

This is a play about two boys who find a kitten. Read the play. Then, answer the questions. On your answer sheet, darken the circle for each correct answer for multiple-choice items. For the short-answer item, write your answer on a separate sheet of paper.

Lost and Found

Characters:

JON LIU, age 9

ANDREW LIU, age 11

MRS. LIU

TEENAGE GIRL

TEENAGE GIRL'S FATHER

SCENE 1

(Jon and Andrew are walking home from school from stage right, chatting about the day at school.)

JON: Did you see the kickball game at recess? *(Stops walking and holds up his hand, listening.)* Do you hear something?

ANDREW: Yeah, it sounded like it was over here. *(Walks to a bush, reaches behind it, and picks up a kitten with a bell on its collar.)*

JON: What are you doing back there, little guy? Andrew, do you think we can keep him? Dad said we could get a cat soon.

ANDREW: Let's go home and ask.

(Both walk offstage.)

SCENE 2

(The boys are sitting on their living room floor, petting the kitten. Mrs. Liu walks in and jumps, startled.)

MRS. LIU: Where did that kitten come from?

ANDREW: We found him behind some bushes down the street.

JON: *(Jumps up and runs over to his mother, eager.)* Mom, look at this sweet little ball of fur! Can we keep him?

MRS. LIU: *(Walks over and picks up the kitten, looking thoughtful.)* He has a collar, so someone was taking care of him. He probably ran outside and got lost. The owner must be looking for him.

JON: Oh. *(Looks disappointed, then perks up.)* But what if no one is? Then can we keep him?

MRS. LIU: *(Hands the kitten to Jon, who hugs it close.)* Well, let's try to find the owner first. Why don't you boys make posters to put up in the neighborhood? I'll put an advertisement in the newspaper tomorrow. If no one claims the kitten, then maybe we'll keep him.

ANDREW: I'll get some paper and markers.

(The stage lights go down.)

SCENE 3

(The boys are outside taping a poster to a telephone pole. The teenage girl and her father walk toward them from stage right, looking from side to side and calling for a cat.)

GIRL: Simon! Here, kitty, kitty, kitty! Aw, Dad, we'll never find him! I should have closed the back door!

FATHER: Well, let's just keep looking. He's probably still nearby.

(Jon watches them approach while Andrew finishes taping the poster. Jon starts to speak, then stops, hesitating, then starts again.)

JON: Umm, excuse me. Are you looking for an orange kitten? One that's really nice and doesn't scratch at all when you pick him up?

GIRL: *(Excited.)* Dad, that's Simon!

ANDREW: I think we found him when we were walking home. Come on, we'll show you. *(Andrew starts to walk away to stage left. Jon doesn't follow. He looks sad.)* Jon, come on! This has to be his owner.

JON: *(To Andrew, in a low voice; girl is watching them and overhears.)* But now I'll never see him again!

GIRL: We live right over there. You could visit him sometimes. He always needs someone to play with while I do my homework.

JON: Really? Wow! You bet I'll come visit!

(All walk offstage.)

13. According to the stage directions, what are the boys doing at the beginning of Scene 1?

   A playing a game of kickball during recess

   B searching for a lost pet on their way home from school

   C talking about the school day as they walk home

   D looking for a lost ball in the bushes

14. What is the setting of Scene 2?

   A the street near the teenage girl's home

   B the bushes on the walk home

   C the school playground

   D the boys' home

15. Why does the teenage girl most likely invite Jon to come over and visit the kitten?

   A She knows that Jon is upset that he might not see the kitten again.

   B She wants to make sure that the kitten will not try to run away again.

   C She needs Jon to help her with her homework.

   D She wants to give the kitten to Jon.

16. What is the main problem in the play?

   A The teenage girl loses her cat.

   B Jon and Andrew bring a kitten home.

   C Jon wants to keep the kitten he found.

   D Mrs. Liu wants to find the kitten's owner.

17. In Scene 2, why does Jon call the cat a "little ball of fur"?

   A to explain how round the kitten is

   B to show how cute the kitten is

   C to explain why the kitten likes to play with balls

   D to describe how playful the kitten is

18. What will the girl most likely do the next time she leaves her house?

   A visit Jon and Andrew

   B look for Simon

   C go for a walk with her father

   D close the back door

19. How do Jon and Andrew react differently when they realize the girl is the kitten's owner?

This poem describes what happens when a person goes fishing. Read the poem. Then, answer the questions. On your answer sheet, darken the circle for each correct answer for multiple-choice items. For the short-answer item, write your answer on a separate sheet of paper.

A Fish Story

The sun shone hot, the sky was blue,

wavelets lapped my new canoe.

I cast my lure and felt a tug;

my rod arced down; the line grew snug.

"A whale!" I hoped. A record catch!

A fish a size no one could match.

A silver streak, a glistening fin,

with all my might I reeled it in.

And soon the dark, cruel face I saw,

with eyes like ice and a gaping maw.

I leaned and looked, his tail thrashed down,

My world went green and wet all 'round.

I lost it all, my rod, my hat.

I'd caught no dinner for all of that.

My fish swam free in all his glory

and had one whopper of a people story.

20. Read this line from the poem.

> My fish swam free in all his glory

What does the phrase "in all his glory" mean?

A with a high level of anxiety

B in frantic excitement

C at the height of success

D in a brief burst of fame

21. In the second stanza, why does the speaker refer to a whale?

A The speaker wants to catch a very large fish.

B The speaker is fishing in the sea.

C The speaker wants to go whale hunting.

D The speaker is fishing from a very large boat.

22. How does the speaker's mood change from the beginning to the end of the poem?

A The speaker's mood changes from discouraged to excited.

B The speaker's mood changes from depressed to happy.

C The speaker's mood changes from hopeful to disappointed.

D The speaker's mood changes from annoyed to cheerful.

23. What is the theme of this poem?

A If you keep trying, you can achieve your goals.

B Things do not always turn out the way we plan.

C It is important to keep a sense of humor about everything.

D People should respect and care for the natural world.

24. Read these lines from the poem.

> A silver streak, a glistening fin,
> with all my might I reeled it in.

Explain the mood these lines create and how the words appeal to the reader's senses.

Name _____   Date _____

In this poem, a girl describes a rainstorm. Read the poem. Then, answer the questions. On your answer sheet, darken the circle for each correct answer for multiple-choice items. For the short-answer item, write your answer on a separate sheet of paper.

The Rainstorm

The air grows cool.

The sun vanishes.

The clouds advance. Brilliant colors

weave together on Earth's ceiling.

Blue, red, yellow, orange.

The thunder bellows.

The leaves rustle.

The wind whistles.

A colossal orchestra

plays its music in Earth's hall.

Rumble, whoosh, hiss, howl.

The clouds unlock.

The water cascades down.

A massive shower

gently cleanses Earth's floor.

Drip, drop, splish, splash.

I dance playfully through the puddles.

I sing along with the symphony's song.

I taste the sweet drops of rain,

a simple bystander

to nature's majestic performance.

Applause, applause, applause.

25. Which characteristic makes this selection a poem?

   A It repeats phrases and lines to create rhythm.

   B It contains a pattern of rhyming words.

   C It uses humor to describe an everyday event.

   D It emphasizes sounds and images to create meaning.

26. What can you tell about the speaker in the poem based on the illustration?

   A The girl is happy because the rain has stopped.

   B The girl is in a hurry to get out of the rain.

   C The girl is not dressed well for the weather.

   D The girl is enjoying being outdoors in the rain.

27. What does the last line of the poem, "Applause, applause, applause," mean?

   A The girl appreciates the rain.

   B The rain makes the sounds of clapping.

   C The girl is clapping for the rain.

   D The girl is taking a bow for her performance.

28. What is the speaker likely to do the next time it rains?

   A play a musical instrument

   B go outside and have fun

   C feel sad about being stuck indoors

   D play a game inside with her friend

29. What does the poet mean by the lines "A colossal orchestra plays its music in Earth's hall"?

   A The sound is made by people playing in the rain.

   B The rainstorm's sounds are like pleasant music.

   C The sounds outdoors are made by musical instruments.

   D The rainstorm's sounds are like loud echoes on Earth.

30. Name three senses the poem appeals to. Give an example from the poem of how the poet appeals to each sense.

Test Tips for Reading Informational Texts

Identifying the Main Idea and Supporting Details

The **main idea** of a selection is the central thought or the most important point. **Supporting details** give more information about the main idea. Sometimes the main idea is stated directly at the beginning of a selection. Other times, a reader must think about the information that is presented and determine the focus or the main idea. Follow these steps in order to identify the main idea of a selection and answer a main idea question.

Step 1: Read the selection and determine the topic, or what the selection is about.

Step 2: Look for the important details in the selection. Think about what the details have in common. The details should point to the main idea.

Step 3: State the main idea in your own words. Then, look for an answer that closely matches your own. Be careful not to select a detail that merely supports the main idea as your answer. Also remember that the main idea reflects the entire selection, not just one paragraph or one section.

Step 4: Check to make sure that the details in the selection support your answer.

Identifying Author's Purpose and Point of View

An **author's purpose** is the reason he or she is writing. Authors may write to entertain, to express ideas, to inform, to instruct, or to persuade. In most nonfiction selections, the author's purpose is to inform, instruct, or persuade. Use the steps below for help in answering questions about an author's purpose for writing:

Step 1: Look in the text for clues such as the ones below.

- illustrations, diagrams, maps, charts, and headings: **to inform or instruct**

- numbered or bulleted lists, steps for doing something, and how-to selections: **to instruct**

- use of words like *should* and *must*, letters to the editor or a person in charge, and use of words that express opinions such as *great*, *poor*, and *outstanding*: **to persuade**

- frequent use of the word *I*, emotional words, feeling words: **to express**

- description that tells a story, dialogue, rhymes, drama, or humor: **to entertain**

Step 2: Look for the response that most closely matches the general purpose you have identified.

An author can also have a particular **point of view** about a topic. A point of view is the way an author sees a topic.

Step 1: Look for positive or negative words when the author describes a topic. Also look for statements about what the author believes.

Step 2: Try to answer the question about point of view in your own words.

Step 3: Look for the choice that best matches your own answer.

Analyzing Text Structure

Text structure is the way in which the author has organized ideas. Understanding the text's structure can help readers follow the writer's ideas. Four common patterns of organization are listed below.

- **Cause and effect** focuses on what causes something to happen and what happens as a result. Some of the clue words and phrases that signal cause and effect are *because*, *since*, *so that*, *therefore*, and *as a result*.

- **Chronological order** is the order in which events happen. Look for words that signal time and order, such as *first*, *next*, *then*, *last*, and *finally*. You can also look for dates of events.

- **Comparison and contrast** writing focuses on how two or more things are alike or different. Some clue words that signal contrast are *although*, *but*, *different*, *unlike*, *however*, and *yet*. Some clue words that signal comparison are *also*, *as well*, *both*, *likewise*, *alike*, *same*, *similar*, and *too*.

- **Problem/solution** writing describes a problem and then offers ideas for how the problem can be solved.

Use the steps below to help analyze text structure.

Step 1: Look for clue words that signal the organization of the selection.

Step 2: Look for important ideas and think about how they are connected.

Step 3: Look for the answer choice that best matches the organization.

Using Graphic Features

Headings, photos, captions, labels, maps, charts, tables, diagrams, and illustrations are all **graphic features**. Graphic features such as headings, captions, and labels are designed to help readers find information. Graphic features such as maps, charts, tables, diagrams, and illustrations present information visually. When a selection includes graphic features, use the steps below.

Step 1: Read the title, labels, captions, and legend.

Step 2: Interpret the graphic. Think about what it shows and what it helps you understand.

Step 3: Think about how the information in the graphic feature relates to the text.

Summarizing a Text

A **summary** includes the most important ideas and details from a selection. A summary should cover the entire selection. Follow these steps to choose the best answer to a summary question:

Step 1: Look for the main idea and the most important supporting details as you read the selection.

Step 2: Consider every answer choice. Get rid of those that retell only part of the selection, make a general statement about the selection but include no important details, or focus on unimportant details in the selection.

Step 3: Be sure that the answer you choose covers the *entire* passage by including the main idea and major supporting details.

Making Inferences

To make an **inference**, you must use details from the selection as well as what you already know to figure something out. Often there are ideas within a passage that the author is trying to convey but does not state directly. Use the following steps to answer inference questions:

Step 1: Skim the passage once for a general understanding; then, reread it carefully.

Step 2: Review each answer choice and think about whether it is supported by information in the selection. Cross out any answers that are unsupported or that do not make sense for the selection.

Step 3: Confirm your answer by using what you already know about the topic of the selection.

Drawing Conclusions

On a reading test, you may be asked questions that begin like this: "Why do you think . . ." or "Based on the information in the passage . . ." Questions like these require you to draw a conclusion. When you draw a **conclusion**, you put together evidence in the passage to support an idea. Use the steps below to respond to these types of questions:

Step 1: Read the question to identify the topic of the question.

Step 2: Study the answer choices, ruling out those choices that are clearly wrong.

Step 3: Reread the passage and look for evidence that supports one of the remaining answer choices.

Evaluating Arguments and Claims

When you evaluate an **author's arguments and claims**, you look for evidence that supports an author's claims. Use the following steps to evaluate arguments and claims:

Step 1: Read the text carefully. Take notes on what the author is saying.

Step 2: Look for details that support the author's ideas.

Step 3: Evaluate the support. Think about why the author supported the argument or claim that way. Also think about other kinds of support the author might have used.

23

Name _____ Date _____

This selection describes a comet, which is a ball of icy particles that orbits the sun. Read the selection. Then, answer the questions. On your answer sheet, darken the circle for each correct answer for multiple-choice items. For the short-answer item, write your answer on a separate sheet of paper.

Halley's Comet

Halley's Comet is expected to be visible again in the United States in the year 2062. The comet passes within sight of Earth only once about every 76 years, so most people only get to see it once in their lifetime.

Edmund Halley was an English astronomer who first saw the comet in 1682. It lit up the night sky for weeks, and many people feared that it would never disappear. People were afraid that the comet would come down on Earth and cause the death of many people. Halley tried to tell the public that they had nothing to fear from the comet. He based his belief on his friend Isaac Newton's fairly new scientific theories on gravity. Using these theories, Halley predicted that the comet would return again in the year 1758.

As Halley predicted, the comet returned in 1758. It was Christmas night of that year. Halley died in 1742, so he couldn't <u>verify</u> the accuracy of his prediction. Because Halley was the person who had correctly predicted the comet's return, people started calling it "Halley's Comet."

The comet came to be called "The Flaming Sword" because of its shape and the many stories about its sighting. Some people started to blame the comet for famine, war, and disease. They thought it was an evil star and an omen of bad events.

1. According to the selection, how were Newton and Halley alike?

   A They both had theories about gravity.

   B They both saw the comet reappear in 1758.

   C They were both scientists.

   D They both saw the comet twice in their lifetime.

2. Which statement is supported by evidence in the selection?

   A Halley was willing to accept new ideas.

   B Halley was not good at proposing scientific theories.

   C Halley was famous during his lifetime.

   D Halley was incorrect in his prediction about the comet.

3. What does the word verify mean in this selection?

   A describe

   B predict

   C confirm

   D support

4. How many times do most people get to see Halley's Comet in their lifetime?

   A once

   B twice

   C ten times

   D seventy-six times

5. Why was the comet named after Edmund Halley?

   A Halley told people that the comet would not fall to Earth.

   B Halley was the first person to observe the comet in 1682.

   C Halley suggested his name to replace "The Flaming Sword."

   D Halley correctly predicted the comet would appear in 1758.

6. Which of these generalizations is supported in the selection?

   A Scientists in the 1600s and 1700s were not very knowledgeable.

   B People were superstitious in the 1600s and 1700s.

   C Comets cause a lot of bad events on Earth.

   D Comets appear more frequently today than they did in the past.

7. What is the main idea of the selection?

Name _____   Date _____

This selection describes George Washington, America's first president. Read the selection. Then, answer the questions. On your answer sheet, darken the circle for each correct answer for multiple-choice items. For the short-answer item, write your answer on a separate sheet of paper.

The Greatest of All

At the top of your list of "Best Presidents of the United States," write the name George Washington. This man did it all. He led the troops to victory in the Revolutionary War. He helped create the Constitution. He served as our country's first president. He even picked the spot for the capital city!

A great president should be admired. People admired Washington so much that some thought that he should be named king. Washington refused that honor.

A great president should face challenges and find a way to triumph over them. Washington faced huge problems. He had to show the states that the federal government was serious about its laws. After all, the United States could not really be "united" if individual states chose which laws to follow and which to ignore.

If you are still unsure about Washington's greatness, think about this. When he ran for a second term as president, he was elected <u>unanimously</u>. That means that everyone voted for him. Clearly, the American people could see the greatness of the man.

So, when you rank presidents, I urge you to remember the fellow who started it all. He was George Washington, and he was the greatest president.

The Life of George Washington

1749		1775		1789
Became a surveyor		Commanded American army		Served as first U.S. President

1730	1740	1750	1760	1770	1780	1790	1800

1732		1758		1774		1799	
Born		Joined House of Burgesses		Elected to first Continental Congress		Died	

8. According to the time line, which event happened first?

   A Washington commanded the American army.

   B Washington was elected to the Continental Congress.

   C Washington became president.

   D Washington joined the House of Burgesses.

9. Why did the author write this selection?

   A to inform readers about the details of Washington's life

   B to entertain readers with amusing stories about Washington

   C to convince readers that Washington was the greatest president

   D to tell a story about how Washington became president

10. Why does the author include information about Washington being elected for a second term?

   A to show that Washington was popular in some states

   B to show that many people considered Washington a great leader

   C to show that Washington always did the right thing for the country

   D to show that Washington should have become king

11. Which type of writing is this passage an example of?

   A biography

   B persuasive essay

   C fiction

   D drama

12. How is this selection organized?

   A by presenting reasons that support an opinion

   B by listing events in the order they occurred

   C by describing a cause and explaining the effects

   D by comparing and contrasting the best and worst

13. What does the word unanimously mean in this selection?

   A by old people

   B by young people

   C by no one

   D by everyone

14. What information in the selection supports the idea that George Washington was a great American leader? Use evidence from the selection to support your response.

Name _____ Date _____

This selection describes how to decorate a box. Read the selection. Then, answer the questions.
On your answer sheet, darken the circle for each correct answer for multiple-choice items. For the
short-answer item, write your answer on a separate sheet of paper.

Decorate a Treasure Box

Materials

- thick drawing paper
- crayons or markers
- small box with lid
- decoupage glue *(available at craft stores)*
- brush
- scissors

1. Cut a piece of paper the same size as the lid of the box.

2. On the paper, draw a picture with crayons or markers.

3. Use a brush to cover the back of the picture with decoupage glue. Place
   the picture on the lid of your box.

4. Let the picture dry for two hours.

5. Coat the picture with another layer of glue, and let it dry overnight.

15. Why are some words in this selection in slanted, or italic, type?

   A to explain the meaning of a word

   B to describe a particular step

   C to tell where to get an item needed for the project

   D to keep the reader's attention from wandering

16. What would most likely happen if you did not first cut the paper the same size as the lid?

   A The picture would be the wrong size.

   B The glue would not stick.

   C You would not have the right kind of paper.

   D The picture would not dry properly.

17. About how long does the project take from start to finish?

   A twenty minutes

   B two hours

   C one day

   D one week

18. Which of the following should you do when making the treasure box?

   A Use two lids.

   B Draw two pictures.

   C Buy two brushes.

   D Use two coats of glue.

19. How is this selection organized?

   A from most important step to least important step

   B in the order you should perform the steps

   C from least important step to most important step

   D by the amount of time each step takes

20. Why does the author probably list the materials for the project at the top?

Name _____ Date _____

This selection describes how to perform a magic trick. Read the selection. Then, answer the questions. On your answer sheet, darken the circle for each correct answer for multiple-choice items. For the short-answer item, write your answer on a separate sheet of paper.

A Magic Trick

I learned a magic trick that will amaze people young and old. You will need the following supplies: a strip of paper about two inches wide by eight inches long, two paper clips, and a rubber band. Follow the steps and refer to the pictures to help you. The pictures are numbered according to the steps.

First, bring one end of the paper to the middle. Secure it with a paper clip.

Second, slip the rubber band through to the middle of the paper.

Next, bring the other end of the paper around to the front to form a loop around the first paper clip and the rubber band. Hold the middle and the front of the paper together with the second paper clip.

Fourth, wave your hand mysteriously over the paper. Say the word "Abracadabra" while you pull the ends of the paper in opposite directions.

The result of the trick should be that the two paper clips will hang together from the rubber band on the paper.

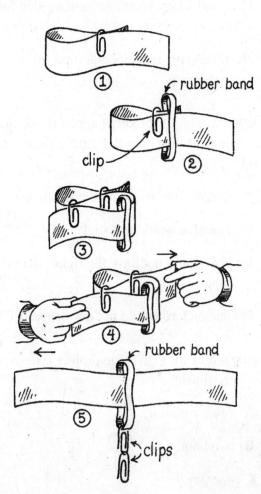

21. Which of the following would be a good title for this selection?

   A The Amazing Linking Clips

   B Loopy Loops

   C Shooting Rubber Bands

   D The Disappearing Paper Clips

22. If the trick is done correctly, what should happen when the ends of the strip of paper are pulled in opposite directions?

   A The paper should rip.

   B The two paper clips should hang together from the rubber band on the paper.

   C The rubber band should stay on the paper, but the paper clips should fly off.

   D The rubber band should fly into the air, and the paper clips should remain on the paper.

23. Why should you wave your hand over the paper in the fourth step?

   A to make people forget that you have a piece of paper

   B to secretly slip the paper clips onto the rubber band

   C to use magic to make the rubber band and paper clips move

   D to convince people you are doing something magical

24. Which of the following should you do first?

   A Hook two paper clips together and hang them from a rubber band.

   B Use a paper clip to form a loop with one end of the paper.

   C Cut a strip of paper two inches wide by eight inches long.

   D Put a rubber band over the middle part of the piece of paper.

25. What does Illustration 4 show?

   A putting a rubber band over the middle of the paper loop

   B pulling the ends of the paper in opposite directions

   C using two paper clips to form two loops in a strip of paper

   D placing a paper clip to form a loop with the rubber band inside

26. Summarize the selection.

Language Arts and Vocabulary
Test Tips and Practice

Standardized Tests for Language Arts

In the Language Arts Practice section, you will review grammar, usage, and mechanics conventions. Then, you will answer multiple-choice questions about these conventions. There will also be some questions that are not multiple choice. For these questions, you will need to rewrite a sentence correctly.

Passage-Based Items

Some of the questions will be based on a passage. Grammar and usage passages will have numbered blanks. You will choose the word or words that best complete the blanks. Mechanics passages have underlined sections. You will determine whether the underlined parts have errors in spelling, capitalization, punctuation, or no errors at all.

As you read a passage, pay attention to things that look or sound incorrect. This might be a misspelled word, an incorrect verb, or words that do not agree in tense or number. You may want to mark anything that seems like an error as you read.

Test Tips for Grammar and Usage

Complete Sentences

A **complete sentence** has a subject and a predicate. If a sentence is missing either part, it is a fragment.

> **Fragment:** Sprinting quickly up the hill.
> **Complete Sentence:** Felix was sprinting quickly up the hill.

A run-on sentence has two or more parts, but the parts are joined incorrectly. To fix a run-on sentence, you can break it into two smaller sentences, add or change punctuation, or rearrange words in the sentence.

> **Run-on Sentence:** I know there's a mouse in the basement, I hear it scratching.
> **Correct Sentence:** I know there's a mouse in the basement because I hear it scratching.

Nouns and Pronouns

A **noun** names a person, place, thing, or idea.

> **Fred** took a **hike** in the **mountains** near our **home** to enjoy **nature**.

A **pronoun** is a word used in place of one or more nouns.

> Hannah wrote a poem. **She** was thrilled when **it** was published.

Verbs

A **verb** is a word that expresses action or a state of being.

> Emily **mailed** a card to her grandmother, who **was** glad to **receive** it.

Verb Tenses

A verb's **tense** shows the time of its action. A verb's tense is shown by adding endings (such as *-ed*), by adding helping verbs (such as *will*, *has*, *had*), or by a combination of endings and helping verbs. There are six main tenses in English.

The **simple present tense** tells about an action happening now or an action that happens often:

> Lakshmi **walks** to school each day.

The **simple past tense** tells about an action that happened at a specific time in the past:

> Lakshmi **walked** to school yesterday.

The **simple future tense** tells about an action that will happen in the future:

> Lakshmi **will walk** to school tomorrow.

The **present perfect tense** uses *has* or *have* and tells about an action that began in the past but is still happening now:

> Lakshmi **has walked** to school every day this year.

The **past perfect tense** uses *had* and tells about an action that began and finished in the past:

> Lakshmi **had walked** to school until the weather turned cold.

The **future perfect tense** uses *will have* or *shall have* and tells about an action that will be completed in the future:

> By November, Lakshmi **will have walked** to school 40 times.

Adjectives and Adverbs

An **adjective** describes a noun or a pronoun. Adjectives tell *what kind*, *which one*, *how much*, or *how many*. *A*, *an*, and *the* are special adjectives called articles.

> Grace picked **big juicy** strawberries at **the little** farm.

An **adverb** modifies a verb, an adjective, or another adverb. Adverbs tell *where*, *when*, *how*, or *to what extent*. Many adverbs end in *-ly*.

> Gina **slowly** circled the parking lot **before carefully** backing into a space.

Subject-Verb Agreement

Singular subjects take singular verbs. Use singular verbs for *each, either, neither, one, everyone, everybody, nobody, no one, anyone, someone,* or *somebody.*

> Mark **sends** e-mails often.
> **Each** puppy **has** its own personality.
> **Neither** of the cars **gets** good gas mileage.
> **Everyone** on the team **prefers** the white uniforms.

Plural subjects take plural verbs. Use plural verbs for *both, few, many,* or *several.*

> **Both** of my parents **work** for the city.
> **Few** children **walk** to my school.
> **Many** of the girls **like** that singer.

Pronoun-Antecedent Agreement

A pronoun refers to a noun or another pronoun, called its antecedent. A pronoun should agree in number and gender with its antecedent.

> When **Laura** went to the pool, **she** brought a friend with **her**.
> **Evan and I** went to Colorado for **our** vacation so that **we** could go hiking.

Use singular pronouns to refer to *each, either, neither, one, everyone, everybody, no one, anyone, someone,* or *somebody.*

> **Each** girl put the gift **she** brought on the table.
> **Neither** of the twins set **her** alarm this morning.
> **Everyone** has finished **his** or **her** assignment.

Use plural pronouns to refer to *both, few, many,* or *several.*

> **Few** of the students did well on **their** test.
> **Many** children brought **their** own lunches.

Frequently Confused Words

Many words in English have similar or the same pronunciations but different spellings, meanings, and uses. Think about the correct spelling and usage of words you see in test items. The following are some examples of frequently confused words:

accept, except	bare, bear	chose, choose	hear, here
hole, whole	its, it's	knew, new	loose, lose
mail, male	meat, meet	passed, past	plain, plane
right, write	tail, tale	than, then	their, they're, there
threw, through	to, too, two	wear, where	your, you're

Test Tips for Mechanics

Capitalization

Capitalize the first word in every sentence.

> The weather is unpleasant today.

Capitalize the pronoun *I*.

> When I went for a walk, I saw a deer.

Capitalize proper nouns.

> On September 2, Joe will take a train from Philadelphia, Pennsylvania, to Baltimore, Maryland, so that he can watch his favorite baseball team, the Orioles.

Capitalize the first word and all important words in the title of a work such as a book, magazine, movie, or TV show.

> I wrote my report on the book *A Wrinkle in Time*.

Capitalize personal titles used with names of people.

> Dr. Wagner spoke to Miss Olsen's class last week.

Punctuation

End marks

Use a period at the end of a statement or request.

> We watched a solar eclipse last year.
> Do not look directly at the sun.

Use a question mark at the end of a question.

> What time does the game start?

Use an exclamation point at the end of an exclamation or command.

> There's a tornado warning!
> Get inside!

Commas

Use commas to separate items in a series.

> We visited Arizona, New Mexico, and Utah on our trip.

Use commas before the conjunctions *and*, *but*, *or*, *nor*, *for*, *so*, or *yet* when the conjunction joins the parts of a compound sentence.

> The club planned a car wash, but the weather was too rainy.

Use commas to set off interrupters.

> Elizabeth, my best friend, is trying to find homes for the cutest puppies.
> Hey, watch out for that tree!
> Dana, however, learned to ski immediately.

Use commas to separate items in dates and addresses.

> Arturo will be old enough to drive on July 12, 2018.
> The address for the courthouse is 50 West Washington St., Chicago, IL 60602.

Use a comma after the opening of a friendly letter and after the closing of any letter.

> Dear Grandma,
> Yours truly,

Apostrophes

Use apostrophes to form possessives. To form a singular possessive, use an apostrophe and *s* at the end of a noun.

> the boy's bike   my mom's car   Don's friend

To form a plural possessive of a word ending in *s*, add an apostrophe at the end. If the plural noun does not end in *s*, add an apostrophe and *s*.

> the orchards' trees   the kittens' fur   the men's jobs

Use apostrophes to form contractions. The apostrophe takes the place of the letters that have been removed.

> he is   he's   had not   hadn't
> we have   we've   you are   you're

Spelling

A few common spelling rules can help you figure out if words are misspelled. Remember that there are always exceptions to the rules for spelling English words.

Silent *e*

In a word that ends with a silent *e*, remember to drop the *e* before adding an ending that starts with a vowel.

> take   taking   irritate   irritation   care   careful

Double a Final Consonant

In words that end with a short vowel and a single consonant, the consonant is usually doubled before an ending that starts with a vowel.

pit   pitted   top   topping   pot   potter

i Before *e*

When spelling words, use the rule "*i* before *e*, except after *c* and in words that sound like *weigh*."

field   brief   relief   weight   ceiling   deceive

Language Arts Practice

Choose the correct word to complete each sentence. On your answer sheet, darken the circle for each correct answer for multiple-choice items. For the open-ended question, write your answer on a separate sheet of paper.

A box turtle is a reptile that (1) in woods and fields. The box turtle (2) a hinged lower shell. It can pull its legs, head, and tail inside (3) shell and get "boxed in." Box turtles eat earthworms, insects, berries, and (4) leafy vegetables. Box turtles belong (5) the same family as lizards, snakes, alligators, and crocodiles.

1. Using the correct form of the verb "to live," rewrite the sentence with blank 1.

2. What word should fill in blank 2?

   A have

   B has

   C had

   D having

3. What word should fill in blank 3?

   A it

   B his

   C their

   D its

4. What word should fill in blank 4?

   A green

   B greening

   C greener

   D greenest

5. What word should fill in blank 5?

   A two

   B too

   C to

   D though

Choose the correct word or words to complete each sentence. On your answer sheet, darken the circle for each correct answer for multiple-choice items. For the open-ended question, write your answer on a separate sheet of paper.

If you like thrills, excitement, and speed, try snowboarding. It is a combination of (6) skateboarding and skiing. You can (7) down mountain slopes doing wheelies, spins, and hops. A snowboard looks like a (8) it is much wider. Both feet are held onto it with bindings. You stand on the board sideways and (9) the direction you want to go. Then, you bend your knees and begin to glide down the hill. You use your toes and heels against the edges of the board to change direction and to stop. After you get the hang of it, you'll become (10) good!

6. What word should fill in blank 6?

A either

B both

C neither

D not only

7. What word should fill in blank 7?

A look

B go

C zoom

D walk

8. What word should fill in blank 8?

A ski

B ski,

C ski, but

D ski that

9. Using the correct form of the verb "to face," rewrite the sentence with blank 9.

10. What word should fill in blank 10?

A kind of

B real

C some

D really

For numbers 11–15, choose the word or words that best complete each sentence. On your answer sheet, darken the circle for each correct answer.

11. The _____ on the grass at the theater in the park.

    A people sits

    B people sit

    C peoples sit

    D peoples sits

12. The restaurant offers people a choice of either soup _____ salad.

    A and

    B nor

    C but also

    D or

13. By noon tomorrow, Keila _____ the marathon.

    A will have finished

    B had finished

    C will be finished

    D has finished

14. After Andrew _____ the letter, he put it in the mailbox.

    A will write

    B wrote

    C has written

    D writes

15. For science class, Lucy wrote _____ report about fossils.

    A her

    B hers

    C their

    D theirs

Answer each question. On your answer sheet, darken the circle for each correct answer.

16. Choose the sentence that is written correctly.

   A You'll need 100 index cards you'll need a colored marker.

   B They been to my school before.

   C Most people have heard of Ben Franklin before.

   D Me and my friend saw a good movie last week.

17. Choose the sentence that is written correctly.

   A Mom told him to come home.

   B I ran more fast of all.

   C Next week I going to the beach.

   D Can you come over earlier then noon?

For numbers 18–20, choose the best way to combine the sentences.

18. Dad put our car up for sale. The car was used.

   A Dad put our used car up for sale.

   B Up for sale our used car was put up by Dad.

   C Dad, he put up our used car for sale.

   D The used car was put up for sale by Dad.

19. Kacy usually jogs four miles. She jogs early in the morning.

   A Usually early, Kacy jogs four miles in the morning.

   B Four miles usually early in the morning Kacy jogs.

   C In the morning early usually Kacy jobs four miles.

   D Kacy usually jogs four miles early in the morning.

20. We wanted to visit our grandparents. We went on a trip.

   A To visit our grandparents, we wanted to go on a trip.

   B We wanted to visit our grandparents, so we went on a trip.

   C On a trip, we wanted to visit our grandparents.

   D We went on a trip, wanted to visit our grandparents.

Name _____ Date _____

Identify the type of error, if any, in each underlined section of the passage. On your answer sheet, darken the circle for each correct answer for multiple-choice items. For the open-ended question, write your answer on a separate sheet of paper.

Circus elephants have been entertaining audiences for many decades.

The most famous "elephant" of all time was Jumbo. Jumbo was
                        21

brought to the United States by P. T. barnum, a world-famous circus
                                    22

owner. The elephant weighted 12,000 pounds and was more than
          23

11 feet tall. When people wanted to describe something very large
                24

they said it was jumbo size. Today, we still use that word to describe
                                                        25

large items?

---

21. What is the error in underlined section 21?

   A Spelling   **C** Punctuation

   B Capitalization   **D** No Error

22. What is the error in underlined section 22?

   A Spelling   **C** Punctuation

   B Capitalization   **D** No Error

23. What is the error in underlined section 23?

   A Spelling   **C** Punctuation

   B Capitalization   **D** No Error

24. Rewrite the sentence with underlined section 24 correctly.

25. What is the error in underlined section 25?

   A Spelling   **C** Punctuation

   B Capitalization   **D** No Error

Identify the type of error, if any, in each underlined section of the passage. On your answer sheet, darken the circle for each correct answer for multiple-choice items. For the open-ended question, write your answer on a separate sheet of paper.

Jove a Greek god, had many sons. He was thought of as being
26   27

cheerful and hearty. Today when we describe someone as being

cheerful, we say that person is very *jovial,* Jove also had a sister
                                    28

nammed Ceres. She was the goddess of agraculture. The word
29   30

cereal comes from her name.

26. Rewrite the sentence with underlined section 26 correctly.

27. What is the error in underlined section 27?

  A Spelling

  B Capitalization

  C Punctuation

  D No Error

28. What is the error in underlined section 28?

  A Spelling

  B Capitalization

  C Punctuation

  D No Error

29. What is the error in underlined section 29?

  A Spelling

  B Capitalization

  C Punctuation

  D No Error

30. What is the error in underlined section 30?

  A Spelling

  B Capitalization

  C Punctuation

  D No Error

Name _____ Date _____

Answer each question. On your answer sheet, darken the circle for each correct answer.

31. Choose the correct sentence.

  A Tim wrote a report about the book "Al Capone Does My Shirts."

  B Tim wrote a report about the book *Al Capone Does My Shirts.*

  C Tim wrote a report about the book "Al Capone Does My Shirts."

  D Tim wrote a report about the book Al Capone Does My Shirts.

32. Choose the correct sentence.

  A Fran, can you wash the dishes tonight?

  B Fran can you wash the dishes tonight?

  C Fran, can you wash the dishes, tonight?

  D Fran can you wash the dishes, tonight?

33. Choose the sentence that is correct.

  A I just wrote a book called The Big Secret.

  B I just wrote a book called "The Big Secret."

  C Jade read a poem called *All About Trees.*

  D Jade read a poem called "All About Trees."

34. Choose the correct sentence.

  A The weather is mild in March April and May.

  B Soccer is the world's most populer sport.

  C Rex my new dog, likes to eat pretzels.

  D I want to learn to ski, but I'm a little scared.

35. Choose the sentence with correct punctuation.

  A Well I learned about how scientists study fossils.

  B Well, I learned about how scientists study fossils.

  C "Well," I learned about how scientists study fossils.

  D Well. I learned about how scientists study fossils.

Answer each question. On your answer sheet, darken the circle for each correct answer.

36. Choose the sentence that shows the correct punctuation.

   A It was too rainy, to go for a long walk.

   B One boys' bike was missing.

   C On Friday, April 15, we'll have a concert.

   D I like salt pepper and mustard on my sandwich.

37. Choose the answer that shows the correct punctuation.

   A Jo asked, "Who wants to play ball?"

   B "Jo asked, Who wants to play ball?"

   C Jo asked, Who wants to play ball?

   D Jo asked who, "wants to play ball?"

38. Choose the sentence that is correct.

   A "Linda did you go to school?" he asked.

   B Everyone's ideas, are worth hearing.

   C We made a salad with lettuce, cucumbers, and carrots.

   D Pleese take off your hat inside the house.

39. Choose the correct word to complete the sentence.

> She used the results to draw a _____ about the experiment.

   A conclusion

   B cunclusion

   C conclushon

   D conclution

40. Choose the sentence that is correct.

   A The Planet Mercury doesn't have any Moons.

   B The Planet mercury doesn't have any Moons.

   C The planet mercury doesn't have any moons.

   D The planet Mercury doesn't have any moons.

Standardized Tests for Vocabulary

In the Vocabulary Practice section, you will review strategies for determining the meaning of unfamiliar words. Then, you will answer questions that ask you to identify the correct meaning of words using context clues; to use prefixes, suffixes, and roots; and to analyze the relationships between words.

Test Tips for Vocabulary

Using Context Clues

One way to find the meaning of an unfamiliar word is to look for context clues in nearby phrases and sentences.

Step 1: Look at the context of the unfamiliar word. See if the words and sentences around it provide clues to the word's meaning.
- Look for definitions, synonyms, or antonyms that give clues to the unfamiliar word.
- Look at how the word is used in the sentence. Determine the part of speech.

Step 2: Use the context clues to make a guess at the unfamiliar word's meaning.

Step 3: Check your definition by inserting it in the passage in place of the unfamiliar word. Remember that your definition should be the same part of speech as the unfamiliar word.

Using Word Parts

Many words are made up of various word parts. The **root** of a word is the part that carries the word's core meaning. Many roots of English words come from Latin and Greek. Knowing the meanings of these roots can help you figure out an unfamiliar word. A **prefix** is added to the beginning of a word to create a new word. A **suffix** is added to the end of a word to create a new word.

Common Roots

Root	Meaning	Examples
-bio-	life	biography, biology
-extra-	outside, beyond	extrovert, extraordinary
-retro-	back, backward	retroactive, retrospect
-sub-	under, lower than	submarine, submerge
-phon	sound	microphone, phonics

Common Prefixes

Prefix	Meaning	Example
dis-	not	disallow
pre-	before	prepaid
re-	again	replay
un-	not	unable
mis-	wrongly	misdirect
in-/im-/ir-	not	irresponsible, immature

Common Suffixes

Suffix	Meaning	Example
-able, -ible	can be done	repairable
-ful	full of	hopeful
-less	without	hopeless
-ness	state of being	willingness
-ion/-tion	act, process	attraction, pollution
-ly	characteristic of	fondly

Identifying Antonyms and Synonyms

Antonyms are words that are opposite in meaning.

hide / expose
gentle / harsh

Synonyms are words with the same or nearly the same meaning.

exciting / thrilling
beverage / drink

Analyzing Multiple-Meaning Words

Some words have more than one meaning and can function as different parts of speech. To decide on the correct meaning of a multiple-meaning word, decide what part of speech it is and look at its context, or the words and sentences around it.

A **quarter** of the students were absent. (meaning "one-fourth")
Paula found a **quarter** on the sidewalk. (meaning "a coin worth 25 cents")

Use these steps to decide on the correct meaning of a multiple-meaning word.

Step 1: Decide what part of speech it is.

Step 2: Look at its context, or the words and sentences around it.

Step 3: Check your definition against the original sentence to see if it makes sense.

Analyzing Connotations and Denotations

The **denotation** of a word is its dictionary meaning. **Connotations** are the feelings and ideas that have become attached to certain words. A word's connotations can be positive or negative. A word with positive connotations makes you think of good things. A word with negative connotations makes you think of bad or unpleasant things.

As you read, think about the word choices an author makes. Do the words make you think of something positive or negative? Compare the connotations in these sentences.

> She lives in a cozy cottage with historic charm.
> She lives in a small old house.

Idioms, Adages, and Proverbs

The words in an idiom have a different meaning than their dictionary definition. To figure out the meaning of an idiom, think about the context and look for clues.

> Reggie was feeling under the weather, so he stayed home from school.

In this sentence, Reggie is not beneath the weather. The idiom *under the weather* instead means "not feeling well."

Adages and proverbs are traditional sayings that people accept as true. Often these sayings contain some truth, wisdom, or insight about people's behavior.

> All that glitters is not gold.
> A watched pot never boils.
> You can't judge a book by its cover.

Understanding Word Relationships

Analogies are relationships between words. You may be asked to complete analogies on standardized tests.

oak : tree = sparrow : _____

A maple   **B** pine   **C** spider   **D** bird

Follow these steps to complete an analogy.

Step 1: Read the first two words. Notice what part of speech they are. In the example, <u>oak</u> and <u>tree</u> are both nouns.

Step 2: Figure out how the first two words are related. In the example, an oak is a <u>type</u> of tree.

Step 3: Look at the third word. In the example, it is <u>sparrow</u>. <u>Sparrow</u> is also a noun. In an analogy, the third and fourth words should have the same relationship as the first and second words. This means you'd want to figure out what a sparrow is a type of.

Step 4: Look at the answer choices. Maple and pine are types of trees. They're not correct. A sparrow is not a type of spider. A sparrow is a type of bird. The word <u>bird</u> belongs in the blank. Oak is a type of tree, and sparrow is a type of bird.

Vocabulary Practice

Read the selection below. Then, answer each question. On your answer sheet, darken the circle for each correct answer.

A spider is not an insect. A <u>true</u> insect has six legs, while a spider has eight. Also, the body of an insect is usually divided into three parts—the head, the thorax or chest, and the <u>abdomen</u>. A spider's body is <u>segmented</u> into only two parts with the head and thorax united. In certain species of spiders, the long legs are jointed so the spider can move in any direction.

The spider's mouth contains fangs that are somewhat similar to the fangs in a snake's mouth. When a spider bites its prey, a drop of poison is injected into the blood of small insects. The tiny amount of poison in most spiders is not enough to harm humans.

The spider has six spinning fingers called <u>spinnerets</u>. The liquid silk is manufactured inside the body of the spider. The liquid is forced through tiny holes in the ends of the spinnerets. When the silk is exposed to air, it hardens immediately.

1. Which definition matches how the word <u>true</u> is used in this selection?

   A to position something so that it is straight

   B factual; not false

   C faithful or loyal

   D real or genuine

2. Based on clues in the selection, what does the word <u>abdomen</u> mean in this selection?

   A a body part located behind the head and chest

   B the chest or thorax of an insect

   C a joint that allows a spider to move

   D the head of an insect

3. What word in the selection means about the same as <u>segmented</u>?

   A united

   B divided

   C jointed

   D move

4. What are <u>spinnerets</u> used for?

   A injecting poison

   B biting prey

   C picking up objects

   D spinning silk

Name _____ Date _____

Read the selection below. Then, answer each question. On your answer sheet, darken the circle for each correct answer.

Air, dust, and clouds are a <u>blanket</u> over Earth. They form a layer that helps protect humans from the sun, but the layer is <u>insufficient</u>. Ultraviolet rays, which are harmful and burning, still <u>penetrate</u> the air and cloud layer. When these rays reach human skin, they can have a harmful effect. Human skin has a substance called melanin that gives some protection from the rays, but not everyone has enough of it. Melanin makes the skin darker, and it soaks up ultraviolet light. People with <u>fair</u> skin have less melanin. Their skin can burn <u>quick as a flash</u>, so they need to protect themselves by covering up when outdoors and using good sunscreens.

5. Why does the author call air, dust, and clouds a <u>blanket</u>?

   A These things keep Earth warm like a blanket.

   B These things are soft like a blanket.

   C These things cover Earth like a blanket.

   D These things are flat like a blanket.

6. Something that is <u>insufficient</u> is—

   A protective

   B too much

   C not adequate

   D burning

7. What does the word <u>penetrate</u> mean in this selection?

   A cut through

   B burn up

   C harm

   D protect

8. Read this dictionary entry for the word <u>fair</u>.

   > **fair (fer)**
   > 1. *adjective* having an attractive appearance
   > 2. *adjective* light in color
   > 3. *noun* a gathering with competitions and entertainment
   > 4. *adverb* in a proper way; correctly

   Which definition matches how <u>fair</u> is used in this selection?

   A Definition 1

   B Definition 2

   C Definition 3

   D Definition 4

9. What does the expression <u>quick as a flash</u> mean in this selection?

   A very bright

   B very hot

   C very often

   D very fast

On your answer sheet, darken the circle for each correct answer.

10. Choose the word that means the same or almost the same as the underlined word.

> We counted the number of <u>segments</u> that divide the body of the earthworm.

A eyes

B sections

C legs

D skin layers

11. Choose the word that means the opposite of the underlined word.

> Tom <u>accepted</u> the invitation for the party.

A refused

B wrote

C planned

D mailed

12. Choose the word that **best** completes the blank.

> Ed is a very _____ person. He bends over backwards to help his friends, and he would give someone the shirt off his back.

A hopeful

B thrifty

C stingy

D generous

On your answer sheet, darken the circle for each correct answer.

13. Read these sentences. Choose the word that **best** completes **both** sentences.

> We need more _____ to build the deck.
>
> Watch the elephant _____ slowly down the road.

A wood

B lumber

C walk

D material

14. Choose the word that **best** completes the blank.

> last : loser = first : _____

A runner

B racer

C winner

D excited

15. Choose the word that **best** completes the blank.

> stove : cook = ladder : _____

A tall

B eat

C climb

D rungs

Writing Test Tips and Practice

Standardized Tests for Writing

In the Writing Practice section, you will read general strategies for answering writing prompts and review graphic organizers that can help you plan your writing. Then, you will learn about responding to three different types of writing prompts: opinion, informative, and narrative. Standardized tests for writing test your ability in five areas of writing: focus, content, organization, style, and conventions.

Scoring the Writing Prompts

Your response to the writing prompts will be scored on a 4-point scale or a 6-point scale depending on your parent's or teacher's preference. The response will be scored for both composition (focus, content, organization, and style) and conventions. If a response cannot be read, makes no sense, has too little information to be scored, or is blank, it will not receive a score.

SCORING ON A 4-POINT SCALE:

A *4-point* response demonstrates **advanced** success with the writing task. The essay:
- focuses consistently on a clear and reasonable thesis or position
- shows effective organization throughout, with smooth transitions
- offers thoughtful, creative ideas and reasons
- develops ideas or supports a position thoroughly, using examples, details, convincing and fully elaborated explanations, or reasons and evidence
- exhibits mature control of written language

A *3-point* response demonstrates **competent** success with the writing task. In general, the essay:
- focuses on a clear thesis or reasonable position, with minor distractions
- shows effective organization, with minor lapses
- offers mostly thoughtful ideas and reasons
- develops ideas adequately and elaborates reasons and evidence with a mixture of the general and the specific
- exhibits general control of written language

A *2-point* response demonstrates **limited** success with the writing task. The essay:

- includes some loosely related ideas that distract from the writer's focus or position

- shows some organization, with noticeable gaps in the logical flow of ideas

- offers routine, predictable ideas and reasons

- develops or supports ideas with uneven elaboration and reasoning

- exhibits limited control of written language

A *1-point* response demonstrates **emerging** effort with the writing task. In general, the essay:

- shows little awareness of the topic and purpose for writing

- lacks organization

- offers unclear and confusing ideas

- develops ideas in a minimal way, if at all, or shows minimal reasoning or elaboration

- exhibits major problems with control of written language

SCORING ON A 6-POINT SCALE:

A *6-point* response demonstrates **advanced** success with the writing task. The essay:

- focuses consistently on a clear and reasonable thesis or position

- shows effective organization throughout, with smooth transitions

- offers thoughtful, creative ideas and reasons

- supports a position thoroughly, using convincing, fully elaborated reasons and evidence

- exhibits mature control of written language

A *5-point* response demonstrates **proficient** success with the writing task. In general, the essay:

- focuses on a clear and reasonable thesis or position

- shows effective organization, with transitions

- offers thoughtful ideas and reasons

- supports a position competently, using convincing, well-elaborated reasons and evidence

- exhibits sufficient control of written language

A *4-point* response demonstrates **competent** success with the writing task. In general, the essay:
- focuses on a reasonable thesis or position, with minor distractions
- shows effective organization, with minor lapses
- offers mostly thoughtful ideas and reasons
- elaborates reasons and evidence with a mixture of the general and the specific
- exhibits general control of written language

A *3-point* response demonstrates **limited** success with the writing task. The essay:
- includes some loosely related ideas that distract from the writer's thesis or position
- shows some organization, with noticeable gaps in the logical flow of ideas
- offers routine, predictable ideas and reasons
- supports ideas with uneven reasoning and elaboration
- exhibits limited control of written language

A *2-point* response demonstrates **basic** success with the writing task. In general, the essay:
- includes loosely related ideas that seriously distract from the writer's purpose
- shows minimal organization, with major gaps in the logical flow of ideas
- offers ideas and reasons that merely skim the surface
- supports ideas with inadequate reasoning and elaboration
- exhibits significant problems with control of written language

A *1-point* response demonstrates **emerging** effort with the writing task. In general, the essay:
- shows little awareness of the topic and purpose for writing
- lacks organization
- offers unclear and confusing ideas
- demonstrates minimal reasoning or elaboration
- exhibits major problems with control of written language

Test Tips for Responding to a Prompt

- **First, read the prompt carefully.** Be sure that you understand exactly what the prompt is asking.

- **Decide what kind of response you are being asked to write. You should ask yourself, "What is the purpose of this response?"** For example, persuasive prompts ask you to support your opinion about something. Narrative prompts ask you to tell about something you did. Informative prompts ask you to give information about a topic.

- Many tests are timed. **Before you begin writing, consider how much time you have.** A general rule is to allow about one-third of the time to prewrite and plan your essay, about one-third of the time to write a first draft, and about one-third of the time to edit the first draft, revise it, and write a final version. As you practice planning, prewriting, and writing, note how much time you spend doing each of these things. This will help you have a better idea of how much time to allow for each task. Remember that the time you spend planning and prewriting makes the actual writing much easier.

- **Next, organize your thoughts.** Write down notes on a separate sheet of paper before actually writing the response. First, determine the main point of your response. Your thesis sentence, or the statement of your main point, should include the general topic as well as the main idea. It should set the tone and catch your audience's attention. Most importantly, make sure it answers the prompt. This will be the anchor to your response. Then, come up with ideas and details to support your thesis sentence. Your ideas should include the major points that you want to cover in your response. Different graphic organizers can help you develop and organize the points in your essay.

- **Write in complete sentences.** Make sure your sentences and paragraphs flow smoothly and stay focused on your thesis sentence. Sentences should come together smoothly to support the main idea and should be arranged in an order that makes sense to your audience. Be as specific as possible when stating your ideas. Make use of transitional words or phrases if necessary. Also, remember to write neatly.

- **Finally, proofread your response.** Check for spelling and punctuation errors. Look for run-on sentences and sentence fragments. Check verb tenses to see if you have used them correctly. Make the necessary edits as neat as possible.

If you follow the above guidelines, you should succeed on the writing section of standardized tests. Remember that practice makes perfect. Read and write as often as possible on whatever subjects you prefer, and you will see that writing responses will eventually come quite naturally.

Graphic Organizers for Writing

Brainstorming Significant Details

A word web can help you identify details about your topic. Write your topic in the middle circle. Then, write words or phrases that come to mind in the outer circles.

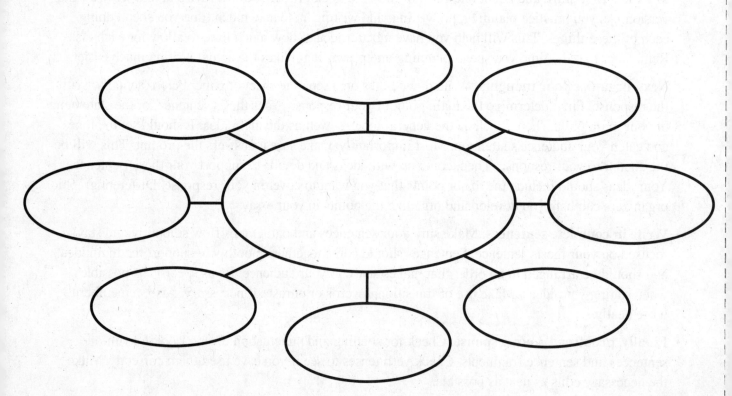

Cause-and-Effect Chart

You can use a cause-and-effect chart to show the reasons something happened (the causes) or the results of an event (the effects).

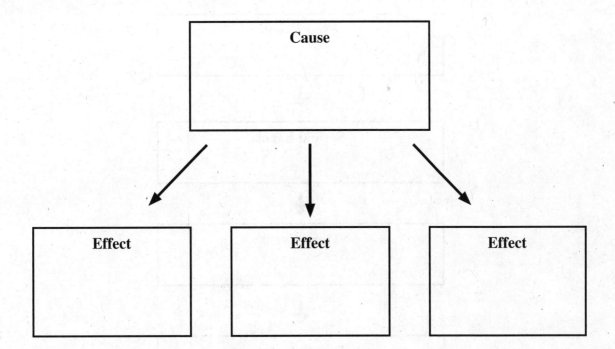

Sequence of Events

A sequence chart is useful if you are writing a narrative that includes different events. The sequence chart can help you identify events and put them in the correct time order.

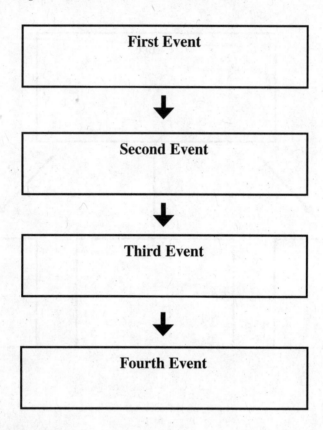

Main Idea and Details

A main-idea-and-detail chart can help you identify your thesis sentence and come up with details that support it.

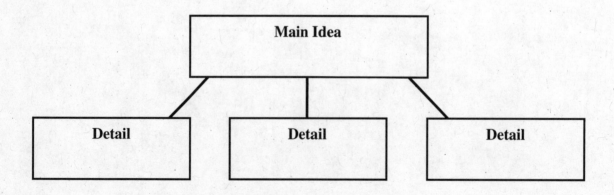

Persuasion

If you need to persuade your reader or express an opinion about an issue, you might want to use this organizer. Write your opinion in the arrow at the top. Then, list convincing reasons and supporting details.

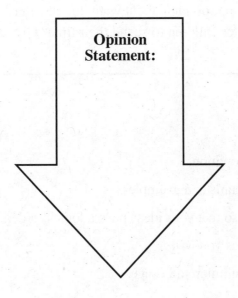

Opinion Statement:

Reason 1:	**Reason 2:**	**Reason 3:**

Support:	**Support:**	**Support:**
1.	1.	1.
2.	2.	2.

Writing Prompt 1: Opinion

Plan, write, and proofread an opinion letter in response to the writing prompt below.

> Many American children watch more than two hours of television every day. Write a letter to a children's magazine expressing your opinion about watching this much television. Do you think this is a good way or a bad way for children to spend their time? Give reasons and information to support your opinion.

As you write your letter, be sure to

- Focus on stating one opinion.
- Explain the reasons for your opinion.
- Support your opinion with details and examples.
- Organize your opinion letter so that your ideas have a logical order.
- Keep your audience in mind as you write.
- Edit your letter for correct grammar and usage.

Strategy for Responding to the Prompt

Prewriting

1. **Analyze the Prompt.** Read the prompt carefully to identify the purpose of and the audience for your response.

Purpose

The prompt asks you to state an opinion about children watching more than two hours of television a day. You will write an opinion letter to a children's magazine explaining what you think about watching this much television each day. Your letter should give reasons and information that support your opinion.

Complete the following sentence:
My purpose is to give an opinion about _____.

Audience

Use the following step-by-step method to analyze the audience identified in the prompt.

Steps	Explanation	Your Response
Step 1 Ask yourself, "Who is the audience for this letter?"	Look at the prompt to find out who you will be writing the letter to.	
Step 2 Ask, "What is my audience going to make a decision about?"	Check the prompt. What decision might the audience make?	
Step 3 Ask, "How can I get my audience to agree with my opinion? What kinds of reasons will help convince my audience?"	Help your audience understand your opinion. What kind of things matter to children your age and younger?	
Step 4 Ask, "How should I address my audience in the letter? What kind of tone and language should I use?"	Remember that your audience is children. Think about the correct way to this audience. What kind of language should you use? What tone will be most effective?	

2. **Brainstorm Ideas.** Use the graphic organizer below to help identify pros and cons of watching more than two hours per day of television. Your opinion should be your own; this will help your writing sound genuine and make it easier for you to write in a convincing manner.

Watching Television Every Day

Pros (reasons for watching more than two hours of television per day)	Cons (reasons against watching more than two hours of television per day)

Name _____ Date _____

3. **Develop Your Idea.** Identify your opinion about whether children should watch more than two hours of television every day. Write your opinion in the center circle. Use the outer circles to brainstorm evidence that supports your opinion and details that you may want to include in your letter.

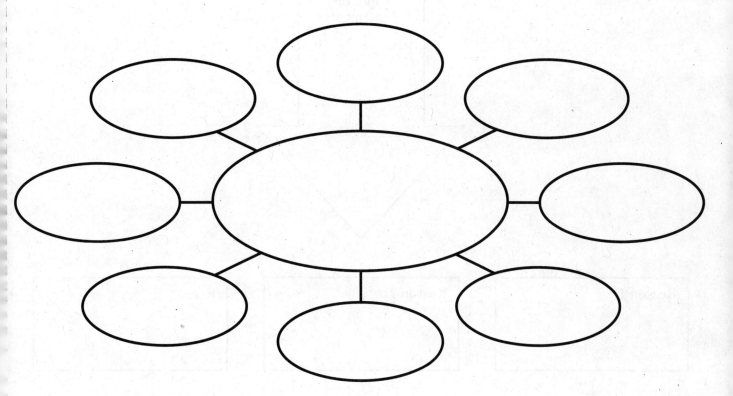

4. **Organize Your Ideas.** Now that you have brainstormed details, organize your thoughts so that you can persuade your audience. In the organizer below, write a thesis sentence that expresses your opinion about watching more than two hours of television every day. Then, add the reasons that support your opinion. Use the information that you brainstormed on the previous page to decide on your strongest reasons. Finally, add details that support these reasons.

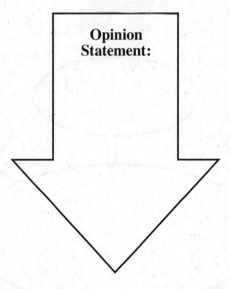

Opinion Statement:

Reason 1:	Reason 2:	Reason 3:

Support:	Support:	Support:
1.	1.	1.
2.	2.	2.

Drafting Your Response

Use the following framework to draft your response to the opinion prompt. Write your draft on your own paper.

Framework	Directions and Explanations
Introduction	
Get your audience interested right away.	To get your audience interested, start with a statement or question that grabs readers' attention.
Give background information.	Provide background on the topic.
Include a clear thesis sentence.	State the focus or point of your letter.
Body	
Explain why you have the opinion.	Explain to your readers why you feel the way you do. How do you think watching a lot of television affects children?
Give reasons and details that support your opinion.	Present your ideas. You can organize your supporting reasons for changing the rule by starting with the strongest reason first, or you can build up to the strongest reason last.

Try to include three strong reasons that support your opinion. |
| **Conclusion** | |
| Remind your audience of your thesis. | Restate your thesis sentence. Remind your readers why they should agree with your opinion about children watching more than two hours of television every day. |

Evaluating, Revising, and Editing Your Response

Use the following strategies to evaluate and revise your response. You may make your revisions directly on your first draft, or, if necessary, write your revised draft on your own paper.

<table>
<tr><th colspan="3">Evaluation Guidelines for Opinion Essay</th></tr>
<tr><th>Evaluation Question</th><th>Tips</th><th>Revision Techniques</th></tr>
<tr><td>1. Does the opinion essay have a clear purpose that addresses the prompt?</td><td>Ask, "Does my response state an opinion about children watching more than two hours of television every day?"</td><td>If necessary, revise your purpose so that it addresses the prompt.</td></tr>
<tr><td>2. Is the response organized appropriately?</td><td>Check for features of a letter, such as a greeting and closing.</td><td>If necessary, revise to make sure your response is in the form of a letter.</td></tr>
<tr><td>3. Does the response include reasons to support the opinion?</td><td>Put a checkmark next to each reason.</td><td>If necessary, think of other reasons that support your opinion.</td></tr>
<tr><td>4. Are the reasons supported by facts and details?</td><td>Lightly underline facts and details that support the reasons.</td><td>Add examples, details, and facts for support.</td></tr>
<tr><td>5. Are the opinion and reasons logically linked?</td><td>Look for connecting words and phrases like for instance, in addition, and in order to.</td><td>Add linking words to show how ideas are connected.</td></tr>
<tr><td>6. Does the response include a strong conclusion?</td><td>Check for a concluding paragraph. Does it restate your thesis or your opinion about the issue?</td><td>Add a conclusion or revise so that the conclusion clearly states your main idea.</td></tr>
</table>

Proofing Your Response

Final Proofreading Guidelines

Proofread your response to ensure that it

- Contains only complete sentences and no fragments.

- Uses proper subject-verb agreement, correct pronoun agreement, and consistent verb tense.

- Uses correct capitalization, punctuation, and spelling.

Draft your final essay on your own paper.

Writing Prompt 2: Informative

Plan, write, and proofread an informative essay in response to the writing prompt below.

> Being fit and healthy is important for people of all ages. Write an informative essay for a kids' health and fitness website that describes things that kids your age can do to stay fit and healthy. Support your ideas with details and examples.

As you write your essay, be sure to

- Focus on the topic.

- Clearly state your main idea.

- Describe things that help make you healthy in detail.

- Organize your writing and present your ideas in a logical order.

- Keep your audience in mind as you write.

- Edit your essay for correct grammar and usage.

Strategy for Responding to the Prompt

Prewriting

1. **Analyze the Prompt.** Read the prompt carefully to identify the purpose of and the audience for your response.

Purpose

The prompt asks you to write about ways kids can stay fit and healthy. You will write an informative essay for a kids' health and fitness website explaining ways to stay fit. Your essay should include descriptive details to support your topic.

Complete the following sentence:
My purpose is to inform about _____ and explain _____.

Audience

Use the following step-by-step method to analyze the audience identified in the prompt.

Steps	Explanation	Your Response
Step 1 Ask yourself, "Who is the audience for this essay?"	Look at the prompt to find out who you will be writing the essay for.	
Step 2 Ask, "What will my audience already know about staying fit and healthy?"	Remember that your audience will be young readers of the website. Some will know more information about your topic than others.	
Step 3 Ask, "What details will matter most to my audience?"	Think about what details you should include. You may not want to tell your audience every possible detail.	
Step 4 Ask, "How should I present the information in my essay?"	Think about things other people your age might care about and can relate to.	

2. **Brainstorm Topic Ideas.** Use the graphic organizer below to help you identify healthy and unhealthy habits and behaviors. Think about what makes them healthy or unhealthy.

Behavior	Healthy or Unhealthy?	Reasons Why

3. **Develop Your Topic Idea.** Use a web graphic organizer to help you brainstorm things kids can do to stay healthy and fit. Write details and examples of healthy behaviors in the outer ovals.

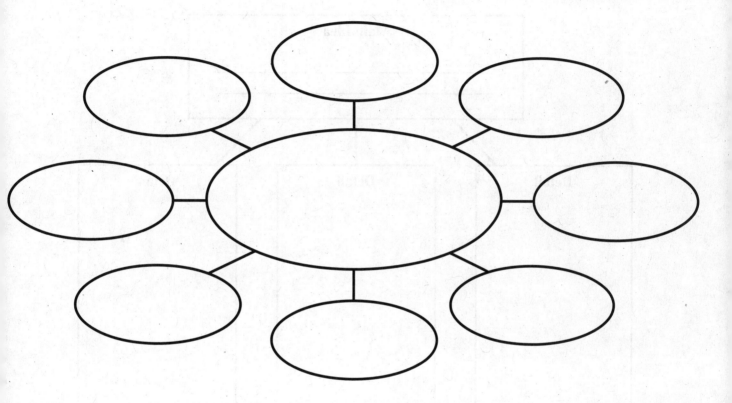

Name _____ Date _____

4. **Organize Your Ideas.** Now that you have brainstormed details, organize your thoughts so that you
    can present them logically. In this main idea organizer, write a sentence describing why it's important
    to be healthy and fit. Fill in the supporting details that explain what kids can do to stay healthy and fit.
    Use the details and examples that you brainstormed on the previous page to help you. Remember that
    you can add more information to the details boxes.

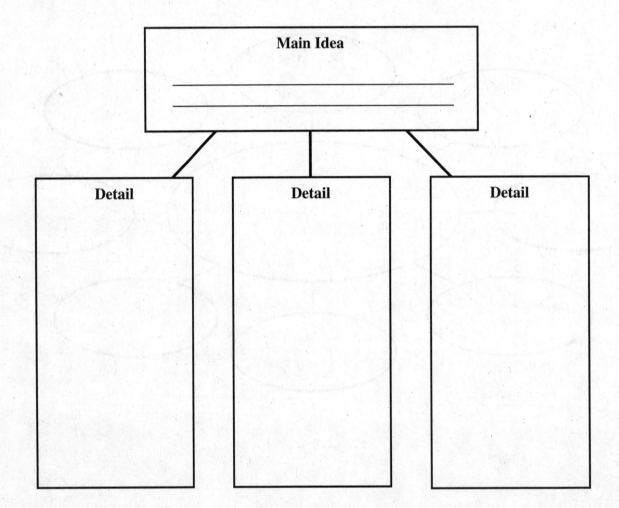

Drafting Your Response

Use the following framework to draft your response to the informative writing prompt. Write your draft on your own paper.

Framework	Directions and Explanations
Introduction	
Get your audience interested right away.	To get your audience interested, start with a statement or question that grabs readers' attention.
Give background information.	Provide background on being fit, such as how it affects children and what they are able to accomplish when healthy.
Include a clear thesis sentence.	State the focus or point of your essay.
Body	
Provide information that explains why being healthy is important.	Help your readers understand why the information in your essay is important and why it should matter to them.
Give examples, facts, and details for support.	Present your ideas. Develop each of your supporting details. Give facts and information that support your ideas.
Present your ideas in a logical order.	Remember to start a new paragraph when you develop a new detail. Use connecting words to show how the ideas are related.
Conclusion	
Remind your audience why being fit and healthy is important.	Restate your thesis sentence and sum up ways kids can stay fit and healthy.

Evaluating, Revising, and Editing Your Response

Use the following strategies to evaluate and revise your response. You may make your revisions directly on your first draft, or, if necessary, write your revised draft on your own paper.

Evaluation Guidelines for Informative Essay		
Evaluation Question	**Tips**	**Revision Techniques**
1. Does the informative essay have a clear purpose that addresses the prompt?	Ask, "Does my response give information about ways to stay fit and healthy?"	If necessary, revise your purpose so that it addresses the prompt.
2. Is the response organized appropriately?	Check that paragraphs are developed and that each paragraph develops a separate detail.	If necessary, break your response into paragraphs and delete repeated information.
3. Do the details you included support the main idea and help readers understand ways to stay fit and healthy?	Put a checkmark next to each supporting detail.	Cut information that is unimportant or off-topic. Add more details if needed to explain your main idea.
4. Do you provide enough examples in your details?	Lightly underline facts, examples, and information.	Add more examples or facts for support.
5. Does the essay have a logical flow?	Look for connecting words and phrases like *another*, *for example*, *also*, and *because*.	Add linking words to show how ideas are connected.
6. Does the response use precise language and appropriate vocabulary?	Identify places where the writing is wordy.	Replace wordy phrases. Choose active verbs and precise words.
7. Does the response include a strong conclusion?	Check for a concluding paragraph. Does it restate your main idea?	Add a conclusion or revise so that the conclusion clearly states your main idea.

Proofing Your Response

Final Proofreading Guidelines

Proofread your response to ensure that it

- Contains only complete sentences and no fragments.

- Uses proper subject-verb agreement, correct pronoun agreement, and consistent verb tense.

- Uses correct capitalization, punctuation, and spelling.

Draft your final essay on your own paper.

Writing Prompt 3: Narrative

Plan, write, and proofread a narrative in response to the writing prompt below.

Life has many challenges. Write a story for a children's magazine about a time you succeeded at doing something difficult. You can write the story about a real experience or an imaginary one. Describe what happened. Develop characters and include dialogue as you describe the events in the story.

As you write your essay, be sure to

- Focus on one topic.

- Include sensory details about the events in your story.

- Explain why the event was difficult.

- Organize your writing and present your ideas in a logical order.

- Provide background so readers understand characters and events.

- Edit your essay for correct grammar and usage.

Strategy for Responding to the Prompt

Prewriting

1. **Analyze the Prompt.** Read the prompt carefully to identify the purpose of and the audience for your response.

Purpose

The prompt asks you to write a story for a children's magazine about a time you succeeded at doing something difficult. The story may be true or made up. The prompt tells you who your audience is and the format for your response.

Complete the following sentences:
The prompt asks me to write a _____.
The purpose of this kind of writing is to _____.
My audience is _____.

Audience

Use the following step-by-step method to analyze the audience identified in the prompt.

Steps	Explanation	Your Response
Step 1 Ask yourself, "Who is the audience for this story?"	Look at the prompt to find out who you will be writing the essay for. Think about who reads a children's magazine.	
Step 2 Ask, "What will my audience expect when they read a school magazine?"	Remember that your audience will need background about the characters and event.	
Step 3 Ask, "How can I keep my audience interested?"	Think about how to tell your story in a clear and interesting way. Do you want to make your story humorous or scary or full of suspense?	

Name _____ Date _____

2. **Brainstorm Story Ideas.** Use the graphic organizer below to consider different topics you might write about. Choosing a story topic that interests you will greatly improve your writing and your ability to develop characters and events.

Something you succeeded at	What happened?	Why was it difficult?

Name _____ Date _____

3. **Develop Your Topic Idea.** Choose the event that you want to write about. Then, identify the characters, setting, and events. The characters are the people in the story. The setting is when and where the story takes place. The events are what happens in the story.

Use the graphic organizer to help you brainstorm parts of your story. Complete the boxes with the characters, setting, and events in the story.

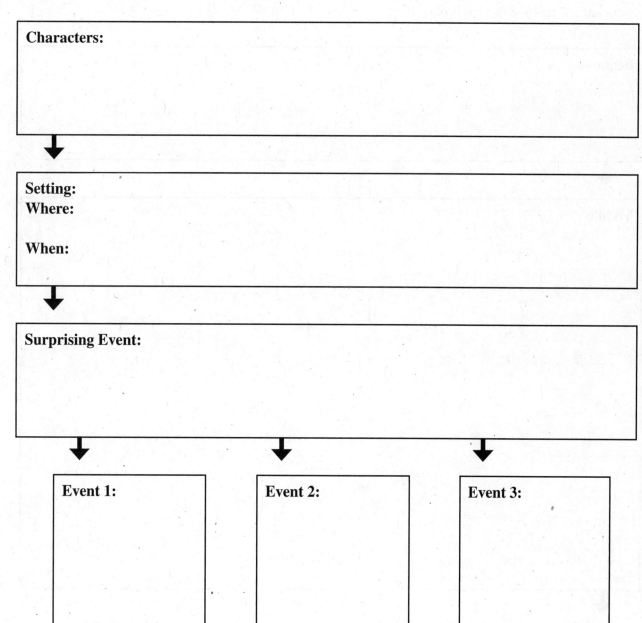

Writing Test Tips and Practice
Higher Scores on Reading and Language Arts, Grade 5

4. **Organize Your Ideas.** Now that you have brainstormed the characters, setting, and events of your story, organize your ideas so that you can tell them in a logical order.

In the graphic organizer below, organize the events of your story into the beginning, middle, and end. The beginning section should describe the surprising event and explain its significance. It should also introduce the characters and setting. Remember to put story events in a logical order. Add details that you want to include in each box.

Beginning

Middle

End

Name _____ Date _____

Drafting Your Response

Use the following framework to draft your response to the narrative writing prompt. Write your draft on your own paper.

Framework	Directions and Explanations
Beginning	
Get your audience interested right away.	To get your audience interested, start with a statement or question that grabs readers' attention.
Explain the difficult experience and why it was important to you.	Tell your readers why the event was difficult for you and what it meant to be successful at it.
Establish the setting and introduce the narrator or characters.	Help your readers understand where and when the story takes place and who is involved.
Middle	
Describe the main problem in the story.	Tell your readers what the main problem or difficult accomplishment is in the story. Explain the event in detail.
Develop characters.	Make your characters believable. Use dialogue and description to make characters come to life.
Present events in a logical order.	Tell events in the order they occur. Use transition words to show how events are connected.
End	
Provide a conclusion to the events.	Explain how the story's problem is solved. Be sure the conclusion flows from the events in the story. Your conclusion should restate why your success was meaningful to you.

Name _____ Date _____

Evaluating, Revising, and Editing Your Response

Use the following strategies to evaluate and revise your response. You may make your revisions directly on your first draft, or, if necessary, write your revised draft on your own paper.

Evaluation Guidelines for Narrative		
Evaluation Question	**Tips**	**Revision Techniques**
1. Does the story tell about an event that addresses the prompt?	Ask, "Does my response tell a story about succeeding at something challenging?"	If necessary, revise your purpose so that it addresses the prompt.
2. Is the response organized appropriately?	Check that events are presented in a logical order, such as the order they happened.	If necessary, reorder the events in your story.
3. Do you introduce a character and events?	Ask, "Who are the characters in my story? What happens to them?"	Cut out unimportant characters or events. Add characters and events if needed to develop the story.
4. Do you develop the characters and events?	Circle details that show what the characters are like. Underline details about the events.	Add descriptive details and dialogue if needed.
5. Does the story have a logical flow?	Look for transition words and phrases, such as *first*, *next*, *then*, and *soon after*.	Add linking words to show how events are connected.
6. Does the response use concrete words and phrases and sensory details?	Identify places where word choices can be stronger, more precise, and more descriptive.	Replace general words and phrases with precise words. Add sensory details that help explain feelings and emotions.
7. Does the response include a strong conclusion?	Check for a concluding paragraph. Does it resolve the story's main problem?	Add a conclusion that logically ends the story.

Proofing Your Response

Final Proofreading Guidelines

Proofread your response to ensure that it

- Contains only complete sentences and no fragments.

- Uses proper subject-verb agreement, correct pronoun agreement, and consistent verb tense.

- Uses correct capitalization, punctuation, and spelling.

Draft your final essay on your own paper.

Reading Practice Test

Literature

This selection tells about a family traveling to the western United States on the Oregon Trail in the mid-1800s. Read the selection. Then, answer the questions. On your answer sheet, darken the circle for each correct answer for multiple-choice items. For the short-answer item, write your answer on a separate sheet of paper.

Promise of a New Life

Russ awoke with a start at the sound of strangers' voices. He sat straight up with his heart racing. Then, he realized that the voices were those of the wagon train's night sentries.[1] Russ and his family had joined the wagon train the day before. Russ was eager to experience his first full day on the trail. He quickly put on his shirt and shoes and hurried to hitch up the team.

Mother was already frying bread over the fire, while his older sister Kathryn carried firewood. Traveling west was Russ's dream come true, but his seventeen-year-old sister looked tired and sullen. She'd left behind close friends and didn't understand why they had to leave their cozy home in Missouri. It was easier for Russ to understand. When people talked about homesteading[2] in a land of roaring rivers and towering trees, Russ felt the same excitement his father did.

Russ looked longingly at the trail, a long snake that worked its way over hills and into valleys. Then, he got the horses in position and began hitching them to the wagon. He had just finished when his father came around the corner of the wagon.

1. sentries: watchers or guards posted at a given spot to prevent surprise attacks during sleeping hours

2. homesteading: claiming and farming land granted to settlers by the United States government in its territories

"Good job, son," he said. Russ looked up and realized that his father was not alone. He was with a dark-haired young man who had a friendly smile. "Come along, Russ. I want to introduce Sam to the family."

The three of them walked toward the small fire where Kathryn and Mother had plates of eggs and fried bread ready for them.

"Sam, this is the Harris family. Everyone, this is Sam Larsen," said Russ's father. "He's traveling on his own and will be taking his meals with us. In return, he'll help me hunt and take care of the animals."

"Welcome," said Mother as she handed Sam a cup of coffee.

Kathryn dished up another plate and handed it to the newcomer.

"I didn't catch your name, Miss," he said, smiling at Kathryn.

"I'm Kathryn," she said shyly.

Russ watched the way Kathryn blushed and smiled down at her hands as she spoke. He thought his sister might find a reason to be happy on the trail, too.

Russ wanted to talk about Sam's life and adventures. Sam seemed to be living out Russ's dreams. "When did you decide to follow the Oregon Trail west?" Russ asked excitedly. "Why are you here by yourself?"

"Well, about two years ago, my family was living in Boston. Dad was out of work when tales of the gold rush in California reached us. He packed up our whole family to head west. We were en route along the Oregon Trail when Mom took sick. My dad and little brother stayed behind to nurse her in St. Joseph, Missouri. I was seventeen, almost a man. I decided to go on to the gold fields alone."

"Weren't you scared to make the trip by yourself?" Russ asked.

"Sure I was, at first," replied Sam. "It wasn't easy. The journey by covered wagon takes about six months through prairies, mountains, and deserts. At times we barely had enough food and water to stay alive. I've lived through floods, Indian attacks, and accidents. I learned to live off the land. I discovered that I enjoyed helping tenderfoots[3] learn the ropes on the trail. It can be lonely at times, but I've met some fine people along the way. Don't have any regrets."

"That's enough for now, Russ," interrupted Mom. "There'll be plenty of time for your questions later. Let Sam eat his breakfast."

Russ wanted to hear more about what life was really like on the Oregon Trail. Next time, though, he'd be sure to have plenty more questions ready.

3. tenderfoots: newcomers to pioneer life in the western United States

1. Why does Russ think of a snake when he looks at the trail?

   A Dangerous snakes live along the trail.

   B The trail looks smooth and dark.

   C Russ is fearful of what the trail will be like.

   D The trail is long and winding.

2. What is the setting in this selection?

   A a farm in Missouri

   B a western desert

   C a trail heading west

   D a cabin in California

3. Which of these is the **best** summary of this selection?

   A Sam Larsen travels west with his family, but they stop in Missouri when his mother gets ill. Later, Sam joins the Harris family on their trip west.

   B Russ, his sister Kathryn, and their parents begin a long journey west on the Oregon Trail. Sam Larsen joins their family, and Russ is fascinated by his stories.

   C Russ has many questions when Sam Larsen joins his family on their trip west. Russ finds out why Sam is traveling by himself and how the journey was difficult.

   D The Harris family joins a wagon train going west. Russ is excited to make the trip, but his sister Kathryn doesn't want to leave their comfortable life in Missouri.

4. From which character's point of view is this story told?

   A Russ

   B Sam

   C Kathryn

   D Mr. Harris

5. Based on information in the selection, why did the travelers most likely use sentries?

   A to watch for floods

   B to stop the horses from escaping

   C to warn of an Indian attack

   D to prevent accidents

6. What does the illustration help you understand?

   A Oxen pulled the wagons.

   B The trail was mostly flat.

   C The wagons couldn't go up and down hills.

   D The wagons traveled in a group on the trail.

7. What sentence **best** describes the theme of this selection?

   A A life of adventure can be dangerous.

   B Sometimes you must face difficulties to reach your goals.

   C Nature can be harsh if you are not prepared.

   D Making new friends is worth the effort.

8. Which of these events happened first?

    A Sam's family learned about the gold rush.

    B Sam joined the Harris family on their trip.

    C Sam's dad lost his job.

    D Sam's mother got sick.

9. What different views do Russ and Kathryn have about the trip? Use information from the selection to support your response.

Name _____ Date _____

This play tells about two friends who work together to solve a problem. Read the play. Then, answer the questions. On your answer sheet, darken the circle for each correct answer for multiple-choice items. For the short-answer item, write your answer on a separate sheet of paper.

A Friend in Need

Characters

JD, *Ravi's best friend*   Mr. Nellore, *Ravi's father*

Ravi, *JD's best friend*   Mrs. Nellore, *Ravi's mother*

Rufus, *JD's dog*

Scene 1

Setting: Front steps of the Nellore home, present day

(JD and Ravi are sitting together. JD's dog, Rufus, is lying between them. Ravi holds Rufus's leash.)

JD:	*(looking sad)* He can't come.
Ravi:	Why?
JD:	What's it called when they think you might have some disease?
Ravi:	Quarantine?
JD:	That's it. The laws in Singapore say Rufus would have to be quarantined for at least a month. I have to find someone to keep him, or else I have to give him away.
Ravi:	*(scratching Rufus under the chin; to JD)*Well, we just have to go to Plan B. *(to Rufus)* Right, buddy?
JD:	Your folks'll say yes, won't they?

(JD looks at Ravi. Rufus chews Ravi's shoelaces. Ravi puts his head in his hands.)

Scene 2

Setting: The Nellores' dining room

(Dinner is almost over. Ravi carries dishes to the kitchen. Mr. Nellore brings a tray to the table.)

Mrs. Nellore: Are you ready for some dessert, JD? Mr. Nellore made his special chocolate cream-cheese brownies.

JD: Yes, thank you. *(Mr. Nellore gives each person a brownie on a small plate.)* That looks good, Mr. N.

Ravi: Mom, Dad, JD and I have something to ask you.

Mr. Nellore: What's that, son?

(JD and Ravi look at each other. Then, Ravi looks at his parents.)

Ravi: If JD can't find anyone to take care of Rufus while he and his family go to Singapore, he'll have to give him away—like he was luggage or something. *(pauses)* So I was wondering . . . can Rufus stay with me? I mean us?

Mrs. Nellore: Well, that's a big commitment. Are you up to the job? Remember, there's no fence around our yard.

Ravi: *(looking to his father)* Dad?

Mr. Nellore: Hmm. Who will look after Rufus while you're at school? He's still a puppy, and puppies chew things. They need lots of attention.

JD: I have some chew toys for Rufus, Mr. Nellore. He's really a good dog.

Ravi: I'll walk Rufus often. I can run home from school at lunchtime to walk him.

Mrs. Nellore: Rufus sheds a lot of hair. I wouldn't want him on my new sofa.

Ravi: I'll vacuum the living room every week, I promise.

JD: Please, Mrs. Nellore? Mr. Nellore?

(Mr. Nellore looks at Mrs. Nellore. Mrs. Nellore smiles and nods.)

Mr. Nellore: Okay, then. Rufus can stay with us while JD and his parents are away. *(in a stern tone of voice)* But you listen to me, young man. *(Ravi straightens up in his chair.)* The dog is your responsibility, not mine and not your mother's. And he absolutely cannot get up on the sofa!

Scene 3

Setting: Ravi's bedroom

(JD and Ravi are sitting on the bed. Rufus is lying on the floor.)

JD: *(looking down)* I guess this is it, then.

Ravi: Hey, keep your chin up! Things will work out fine.

JD: Listen, Ravi, you're the best! I was really worried that. . .

Ravi: *(interrupting)* Really, it's okay. I mean, what are friends for? I'd miss
                   Rufus too, if he were gone. Rufus is like family.

Mrs. Nellore: *(calling from offstage)* Ravi? JD? Hurry up, guys. JD's parents say it's
                   time to leave for the airport.

(JD picks up Rufus, hugs him, and hands him to Ravi.)

JD: Thanks, Ravi. Thanks for everything. See you later! *(As Ravi watches, JD
                   leaves the room. Rufus wiggles and whines, and then licks Ravi's face.)*

---

10. In Scene 3, what does the phrase "keep your chin up" mean?

   A Stay positive.

   B Don't look down.

   C Stand up straight.

   D Don't get distracted.

11. Which of the following shows that "A Friend in Need" is a play?

   A It has characters and settings.

   B It includes spoken parts and stage directions.

   C Its story describes events that could really happen.

   D Its plot has a problem and a solution.

12. Why did the author most likely change the setting from Scene 1 to the Nellores' dining room in Scene 2?

   A to allow JD to leave for Singapore

   B to introduce Ravi and JD

   C to allow Ravi and JD to have a private conversation

   D to introduce Ravi's parents

13. Why can't JD bring Rufus with him to Singapore?

   A The trip to Singapore is too long for a puppy.

   B The airline does not allow dogs to fly on the airplane.

   C Rufus might carry a disease to Singapore.

   D Rufus sheds a lot of hair and chews on things.

14. What is the theme of this play?

   A Friends can work together to solve problems.

   B People must accept responsibility for their actions.

   C It is important to treat others fairly.

   D Dogs are loyal and loving companions.

15. What will most likely happen when JD returns from Singapore?

   A JD will get a new puppy.

   B Ravi will return Rufus to JD.

   C JD will help Ravi build a fence around the yard.

   D Ravi will put Rufus in quarantine.

16. In Scene 2, why does Ravi refer to luggage when discussing Rufus?

   A Ravi thinks Rufus is heavy like a piece of luggage.

   B Ravi is explaining how Rufus is the same color as a piece of luggage.

   C Ravi doesn't want Rufus to be treated like a piece of luggage.

   D Ravi is pointing out how Rufus can sit quietly out of the way like a piece of luggage.

17. What are Ravi's parents like? Provide examples from the play to support your response.

Name _____ Date _____

This poem describes what a man sees when his family goes for a picnic. Read the poem.
Then, answer the questions. On your answer sheet, darken the circle for each correct answer for
multiple-choice items. For the short-answer item, write your answer on a separate sheet of paper.

The Ants

Single file they <u>march</u> along

like an army of tiny bulldozers.

Beneath the tall tree, on a grassy hill

the construction workers build a nest.

They tunnel carefully through the ground

and make a place for each to rest.

They take their orders from a bossy queen,

each doing its part without complaint.

The ants work hard to move the soil,

I can't believe they move so quick.

I just wish they didn't build their nest

so close to my family's picnic!

18. Which statement **best** describes the rhyme pattern in the poem?

   A The poet does not use rhyming words.

   B Each pair of lines ends with rhyming words.

   C The second, fourth, and sixth lines of each stanza end with rhyming words.

   D The fourth and sixth lines of each stanza end with rhyming words.

19. How does the speaker in the poem view the ants?

   A with joy

   B with concern

   C with fear

   D with fascination

20. Why does the poet use the word march to describe how the ants move?

   A to help the reader picture a parade

   B to explain how the ants walk in rows

   C to show that they move in an orderly way

   D to describe the sounds the ants make as they move

21. Which of these lines from the poem contains an example of personification?

   A They tunnel carefully through the ground

   B They take their orders from a bossy queen

   C The ants work hard to move the soil

   D I can't believe they move so quick

22. What does the illustration help you understand?

   A The queen is leading the ants as they search for food.

   B The family is having their picnic on top of the ants' nest.

   C The ants have already discovered the family's picnic.

   D The ants are not interested in human food.

23. In the first stanza, the poet uses a metaphor to compare the ants to

   A construction workers.

   B tunnels.

   C nests.

   D places to rest.

24. Why does the speaker most likely wish the ants built their nest somewhere else?

    A He thinks the ants will bite him.

    B The ants may become a nuisance.

    C He is afraid of insects.

    D The ants might damage the tree's roots.

25. Why does the poet refer to the ants as "an army of tiny bulldozers"?

    A to describe how they fight

    B to explain the sounds they make

    C to show how they move the soil

    D to tell how small their bodies are

26. How does the speaker in the poem feel about the ants? Provide examples from the poem to support your response.

Name _____ Date _____

This selection tells about Mary McLeod Bethune, an African American educator. Read the selection. Then, answer the questions. On your answer sheet, darken the circle for each correct answer for multiple-choice items. For the short-answer item, write your answer on a separate sheet of paper.

Mary McLeod Bethune

Mary McLeod Bethune was born in Mayesville, South Carolina, in 1875. Although young Mary was born free, her parents had been slaves. She grew up working hard in the cotton fields. Then one day, a woman stopped by the home of young Mary to announce that she was starting a school in town and wanted the children to attend.

Young Mary's parents could afford to send only one child to school. They chose Mary. She had to walk ten miles to school and back each day, but she did it gladly. Each night, she taught what she had learned that day to her family. She excelled at her studies and won a scholarship to Scotia Seminary in North Carolina. Later, she won a second scholarship to Moody Bible Institute in Chicago, Illinois.

When Mary graduated, she wanted to become a missionary in Africa. Officials told her that there were no jobs there for African Americans. Upset and disappointed, she became determined to fight against such inequality.

Upon her return to the South to become a teacher, Mary married Albertus Bethune. Later, she accepted a position managing a school and the Bethunes moved to Florida.

Bethune's real desire, however, was to open her own school. She dreamed of educating African American girls so that they would have freedom and opportunity in their lives. Bethune went to Daytona, Florida, and fixed up an old, rundown house. With almost no money, she opened her school in 1904.

Bethune's school started with five students. In just a few years, however, the number of students increased to 400. The school grew to include fourteen buildings. In 1923, the school joined with a men's school to become Bethune-Cookman College.

Bethune also worked on many other projects. She worked to help African American women get the right to vote. She was elected to many groups that supported education and civil rights. She founded the National Council of Negro Women. The president of the United States, Franklin Delano Roosevelt, made her a special advisor for race relations.

In 1936, Bethune was chosen to lead the Division of Negro Affairs of the National Youth Administration. She was the first African American woman to become the head of a federal agency. She became a friend of First Lady Eleanor Roosevelt. They worked together to help African American women, to support education, and to fight against the unfair separation of people based on the color of their skin.

Before Bethune died in 1955, she was honored many times. She was the first African American to get an honorary degree from a southern college. A statue of Bethune now stands in Washington, D.C. It honors the woman who believed that every child deserves a chance to learn.

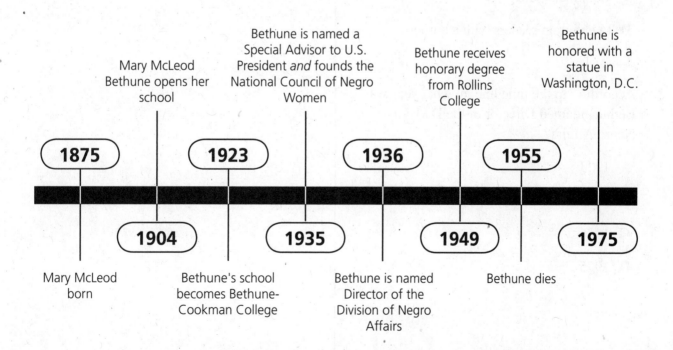

Bethune is named a Special Advisor to U.S. President *and* founds the National Council of Negro Women

Mary McLeod Bethune opens her school

Bethune receives honorary degree from Rollins College

Bethune is honored with a statue in Washington, D.C.

1875   **1923**   **1936**   **1955**

1904   **1935**   **1949**   **1975**

Mary McLeod born

Bethune's school becomes Bethune-Cookman College

Bethune is named Director of the Division of Negro Affairs

Bethune dies

1. What made Mary McLeod Bethune want to fight racial discrimination?

   A She was not permitted to teach in American schools.

   B She was not allowed to attend college in the United States.

   C She was not allowed to be a missionary in Africa.

   D She was not able to afford to go to school as a child.

2. What is the author's purpose for writing this selection?

   A to describe daily life for African Americans after slavery

   B to tell how a woman worked for freedom and opportunity

   C to teach readers the history of Bethune-Cookman College

   D to entertain readers with a humorous story

3. According to the time line, in what year was Bethune named Director of the Division of Negro Affairs?

   A 1923

   B 1935

   C 1936

   D 1975

4. What does the word <u>inequality</u> mean in this selection?

   A unfair treatment

   B upsetting behavior

   C high unemployment

   D cowardly actions

5. What was Bethune's real desire?

   A to open a school of her own

   B to move to Africa

   C to become president of the United States

   D to teach in Washington, D.C.

6. What is the main idea of this selection?

   A Born to parents who had been slaves, Mary McLeod Bethune picked cotton as a child and later earned scholarships.

   B The child of former slaves, Mary McLeod Bethune opened a school and spent her life working to help African Americans.

   C Mary McLeod Bethune was born in South Carolina in 1875 and died in 1955 after being honored many times.

   D Mary McLeod Bethune opened a school in 1904 with very little money, and soon the school grew to have many students and buildings.

7. What is the main way information in this selection is organized?

   A by comparison

   B by cause and effect

   C by problem and solution

   D by time order

8. What evidence **best** supports the idea that people recognized the great contributions Bethune made?

   A She worked hard in the cotton fields.

   B She received many honors.

   C She worked on many educational projects.

   D Her school grew from five students to 400 students.

9. What contributions did Mary Bethune make to civil rights? Identify two contributions in your response.

This selection describes how to make a tool to measure rainfall. Read the selection. Then, answer the questions. On your answer sheet, darken the circle for each correct answer for multiple-choice items. For the short-answer item, write your answer on a separate sheet of paper.

Measuring the Rain

You will need:

• a glass or plastic container, with a flat bottom and straight sides, that is at least 5 inches high

• a small funnel

• a strip of paper 2 inches wide and 5 inches high

• a ruler

• a waterproof marker

• clear packing tape

• a notebook

• a pencil

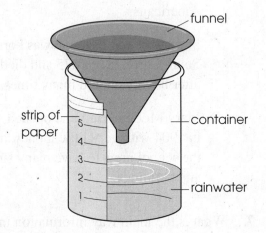

What to do:

1. Make a scale for your rain gauge. First, cut a strip of paper about 2 inches wide and 5 inches high. Then, use the ruler and the waterproof marker to make 1-inch marks, from 1 to 5, on the strip of paper.

2. Attach the paper to a glass or plastic container with clear packing tape. The 1-inch mark should be at the bottom of the container; the 5-inch mark should be at the top. Then, be sure to completely cover the scale with tape to keep it from getting wet. Finally, set the funnel inside the container.

3. Place your rain gauge on a level surface in an open area that is clear of buildings, tree branches, and sprinklers.

4. Check the gauge each day at the same time. Use the scale on the side of the container to determine the number of inches of rainfall.

5. Record the amount of new rainfall in your notebook along with the date and time of day.

6. After you record the information each day, pour out the water in the container so that the gauge will be ready for the next rainfall.

7. When you have measured rainfall for one month, add up all of the daily totals in your notebook. Then, divide that number by the number of days you took measurements. Record the result in your notebook.

What is the result?

You divide the sum of the daily totals for the month by the number of days in the month. The answer shows the average number of inches of rainfall per day for that month.

What does a rain gauge do?

Rain gauges measure the amount of rain that falls during a certain period of time. Water collects in the gauge when there is enough rainfall to measure.

Most rain gauges collect water in a storage container, and a scale or ruler measures the amount of rainfall. Some more complicated gauges weigh the water. One method of measuring rainfall involves the use of radar. Radio waves are reflected, or echoed, by raindrops. These echoes look like spots of light on a radar screen. Bright spots mean large raindrops, and paler spots mean small raindrops. This method is particularly useful for very small amounts of rain that other gauges miss.

Why measure rainfall?

Scientists measure rainfall with rain gauges in thousands of places around the world. They use the measurements to help calculate the average daily, monthly, and yearly amounts of rain in each region. Using the averages, scientists can see patterns of rainfall over time in a specific area or note differences among regions. Understanding rainfall patterns helps many people. For example, farmers rely on this knowledge to plan irrigation for crops. Scientists record rainfall patterns for many reasons. They want to know more about weather changes in different parts of the world, and they try to understand how dangerous storms develop.

Total average rainfall for the whole world is about 34 inches a year, but the amount differs from place to place. Mount Waialeale, in the state of Hawaii, has an annual average rainfall of 460 inches, the highest in the world. The lowest annual average rainfall in the world was recorded in Arica, Chile, at less than 1 inch.

Who made the first rain gauge?

Historians think the first rain gauge was invented in about 1441 in what is now the country of Korea. Two hundred years later, Christopher Wren invented a tipping bucket rain gauge in England.

10. Which step belongs in the empty box?

| Tape the paper to the container. |

| |

| Check the gauge each day. |

A Make a scale on the strip of paper.

B Pour out the water after recording information.

C Average the amount of monthly rainfall in a notebook.

D Place the gauge on a level surface.

11. What is the most likely reason the author asks questions in the headings?

A to show the reader that she is unsure about rain gauges

B to get readers to provide answers

C to help the reader better understand the directions

D to keep the reader interested in the selection

12. Which sentence **best** tells the main idea of the selection?

A Rain gauges are placed in thousands of places around the world to record regional rainfall patterns.

B Rain gauges can measure water three different ways: by collecting it, by weighing it, and by using radar.

C Rain gauges can be made from simple materials and are used to understand weather patterns.

D Rain gauges may have been invented centuries ago in what is now Korea.

13. According to the diagram, which statement must be true about the container used for the rain gauge?

A It must be no more than 5 inches tall so that measurements are accurate.

B It must be wider than the funnel so that the gauge can catch the rain.

C It must be made of clear material so that the water level can be seen.

D It must have very thick sides so that the wind does not blow it over.

14. Based on information in the selection, what is the main benefit of measuring rainfall?

   A Measuring rainfall shows scientists the areas where there will be less than 1 inch of rainfall each year.

   B Measuring rainfall helps us care for crops and plan for dangerous weather.

   C Measuring rainfall protects farmers from drought and keeps them from having to irrigate crops.

   D Measuring rainfall tells us where we can find the highest level of rainfall in the world.

15. In Step 3, why is it probably important to put the gauge in an area without buildings, trees, or sprinklers?

   A It is easier to measure the amount of water in the rain gauge in an open space.

   B Less rain falls in areas where there are buildings, trees, and sprinklers.

   C The objects create breezes that can blow extra water into the gauge.

   D The objects could affect the amount of water falling into the gauge.

16. Which place has the highest rainfall in the world?

   A Hawaii

   B Chile

   C Korea

   D England

17. What does irrigation mean in this selection?

   A bringing water to dry land

   B increasing the amount of rainfall

   C growing crops that need little water

   D measuring the amount of water in the soil

18. Explain what might happen if Step 2 of the directions for making the rain gauge is not followed correctly.

Language Arts and Vocabulary
Practice Test

Language Arts Practice Test

Choose the correct word or words to complete each sentence. On your answer sheet, darken the circle for each correct answer for multiple-choice items. For the open-ended question, write your answer on a separate sheet of paper.

A long line of covered vehicles drawn by slow plodding (1) closer. Beside the wagons, armed men (2) cautiously. The wagons held not only women and children, (3) furniture and supplies. In the rear (4) a guard of six men. This was the (5) wagon train.

1. What word should fill in blank 1?

   A has

   B oxen drew

   C drips

   D leaks

2. Using the correct form of the verb "to walk," rewrite the sentence with blank 2.

3. What word should fill in blank 3?

   A neither

   B also

   C but also

   D nor

4. What word should fill in blank 4?

   A there are

   B are

   C were

   D was

5. What word should fill in blank 5?

   A famous

   B more famous

   C fame

   D most famous

Choose the correct word or words to complete each sentence. On your answer sheet, darken the circle for each correct answer for multiple-choice items. For the open-ended question, write your answer on a separate sheet of paper.

> The (6) way to explore is to go hiking. Going hiking on foot (7) fun. You bring only what you can carry on your back. Before you go hiking, gather some basic gear. You'll need (8) shoes or boots. Take some energy bars and a bottle of water. Put all (9) gear into a (10) a compass so you won't get lost.

6. What word should fill in blank 6?

   A best

   B better

   C bestest

   D bester

7. What word should fill in blank 7?

   A has been

   B was

   C is

   D will be

8. Using the correct form of the word "comfort," rewrite the sentence with blank 8.

9. What word should fill in blank 9?

   A you're

   B you

   C your

   D yore

10. What word should fill in blank 10?

   A backpack. Also

   B backpack, also

   C backpack, also take

   D backpack. Also take

For numbers 11–15, choose the word or words that best complete each sentence. On your answer sheet, darken the circle for each correct answer.

11. The family _____ in the house for a year before they got a dog.

   A will have lived

   B is living

   C has lived

   D had lived

12. The Thompsons _____ to the beach for the holiday next week.

   A driving

   B will drive

   C are driven

   D drive

13. The sandwich came with neither chips _____ a drink.

   A either

   B or

   C nor

   D and

14. During the hurricane there were _____ strong winds but also heavy rains.

   A not only

   B either

   C neither

   D also

15. Melissa brought her umbrella because _____ thought it might storm.

   A he

   B she

   C her

   D it

Answer each question. On your answer sheet, darken the circle for each correct answer.

16. Choose the **best** way to combine the following sentences.

> Randy's shirt got torn. The shirt was caught on a tree branch.

  A Randy's shirt got torn caught on a tree branch.

  B When it got caught on a tree branch, so Randy's shirt got torn.

  C Randy's shirt got torn when it was caught on a tree branch.

  D Whenever Randy's shirt got torn, then it was caught on a tree branch.

17. Choose the **best** way to combine the following sentences.

> The truck dumped a load of gravel. The gravel was dumped onto the driveway.

  A Onto the driveway was a load of gravel dumped by the truck.

  B A load of gravel was dumped by a truck onto the driveway.

  C The truck dumped a load of gravel onto the driveway.

  D The truck, it dumped onto the driveway a load of gravel.

18. Choose the **best** way to combine the following sentences.

> Where is the stamp? It's the one I asked you to put on the letter.

  A The stamp that I asked you to put on the letter, where is it?

  B Where is the stamp that I asked you to put on the letter?

  C Where is it, the stamp that's the one I asked you to put on the letter?

  D The stamp that I asked you to put on the letter, it is where?

19. Find the sentence that is written correctly.

  A Someone's car is in the weigh.

  B Big and small dogs splashing in the pond.

  C Me and my sister loved the movie.

  D Our neighbors leave the lights on all night.

20. Choose the **best** word or words to complete the sentence.

> The floorboards in the old house creaked and _____ all night.

  A groaned

  B made noise

  C squawked

  D sounded

Identify the type of error, if any, in each underlined section. On your answer sheet, darken the circle for each correct answer for multiple-choice items. For the open-ended question, write your answer on a separate sheet of paper.

Just after breakfast <u>on Saturday, we heard a low</u> humming sound in our
                                   21

driveway. <u>It was followed by an, unusual, squeaky car horn.</u> <u>Aunt Jane has a</u>
                    22   23

<u>new car!"</u> my sister shouted. We all rushed out to <u>see Aunt Janes new car.</u>
                                                              24

Her "new" car was more than 50 years old. <u>It was a beutiful 1938</u> roadster.
                                                       25

Its bright green surface shimmered in the sunlight.

21. What is the error in underlined section 21?

  A Spelling

  B Capitalization

  C Punctuation

  D No Error

22. Rewrite the sentence with underlined section 22 correctly.

23. What is the error in underlined section 23?

  A Spelling

  B Capitalization

  C Punctuation

  D No Error

24. What is the error in underlined section 24?

  A Spelling

  B Capitalization

  C Punctuation

  D No Error

25. What is the error in underlined section 25?

  A Spelling

  B Capitalization

  C Punctuation

  D No Error

Identify the type of error, if any, in each underlined section. On your answer sheet, darken the circle for each correct answer for multiple-choice items. For the open-ended question, write your answer on a separate sheet of paper.

Did you ever walk into a kitchen just before <u>a special feast! The</u>
                                                          26

cook may approach you as you enter. <u>"Here sample this," he might</u>
                                                          27

<u>say.</u> Then, you are treated to a sweet taste of a <u>desert sauce, a tasty</u>
                                                          28

<u>sample</u> of rich chocolate, or a yummy mouthful of <u>fresh beets. maybe</u>
                                                          29

<u>you'll get to taste some, fresh, warm, bread. You</u> might be
                              30

full before dinner is even ready!

---

26. What is the error in underlined section 26?

   A Spelling

   B Capitalization

   C Punctuation

   D No Error

27. Rewrite the sentence with underlined section 27 correctly.

28. What is the error in underlined section 28?

   A Spelling

   B Capitalization

   C Punctuation

   D No Error

29. What is the error in underlined section 29?

   A Spelling

   B Capitalization

   C Punctuation

   D No Error

30. What is the error in underlined section 30?

   A Spelling

   B Capitalization

   C Punctuation

   D No Error

Answer each question. On your answer sheet, darken the circle for each correct answer.

31. Choose the correct sentence.

   A Will you visit me? asked Mea.

   B "Will you visit me? asked Mea."

   C "Will you visit me?" "asked Mea."

   D "Will you visit me?" asked Mea.

32. Choose the answer that shows the correct punctuation.

   A Megan please close the door.

   B Megan, please close the door.

   C Megan, please, close the door.

   D "Megan," "please close the door."

33. Choose the sentence that is correct.

   A Sheri is writing a poem called "My Favorite Things."

   B Sheri is writing a poem called My Favorite Things.

   C Sheri is writing a poem called My favorite things.

   D Sheri is writing a poem called "My Favorite Things."

34. Choose the correct word to complete the sentence.

   My friend says that anything is _____.

   A posable

   B posible

   C possable

   D possible

35. Choose the answer that shows the correct punctuation.

   A No, I don't have any money left.

   B No, I don't, have any money left.

   C No I don't have any money, left.

   D No I don't have any, money left.

Answer each question. On your answer sheet, darken the circle for each correct answer.

36. Choose the sentence that is correct.

   A Take off your hat inside the house please.

   B On Friday, October 9, we'll go to the movie.

   C Have you ever traveled by light rail.

   D Who won the nobel peace prize this year?

37. Choose the correct words to complete the sentence.

> Randall's favorite book is _____

   A "Where the Red Fern Grows."

   B Where the Red Fern Grows.

   C *Where the Red Fern Grows.*

   D "*Where the Red Fern Grows.*"

38. Choose the correct word to complete the sentence.

> My dentist recommends that I brush my _____ after every meal.

   A teath

   B tethe

   C teethe

   D teeth

39. Choose the sentence that is correct.

   A Dr. Sarah Brown is the principal of the new school.

   B Sam asked where is my mom.

   C Was she at the birthday party!

   D The restaurant offers fries salad and soup.

Vocabulary Practice Test

Read the selection below. Then, answer the questions. On your answer sheet, darken the circle for each correct answer.

Did you ever think about the ways that dogs and wolves are alike? How might they be related? One theory is that cave dwellers admired wolves for their strength, their speed, and the way they hunted. The cave dwellers decided to train wolves to help them hunt.

Through many centuries of breeding, taming, and training, wolves have developed into the domesticated dogs of today. Dogs still have many characteristics that they inherited from their ancestors, the wolves. For example, dogs bury bones. Wolves bury food and bones when food is scarce. Wolves are hunters. Some breeds of dogs are trained to be hunters because of their unusually good sense of sight, smell, and hearing. Wolves, too, rely on these senses when they hunt. Wolves protect their packs and territories. Some breeds of dogs, such as sheepdogs, can herd and protect flocks of sheep. Both wolves and dogs bark, although wolves don't bark as often as dogs.

All dogs, no matter which breed, began as wolves. It's hard to imagine that even the tiniest Chihuahua has a wolf in its family tree.

1. What does the word admired help you understand about the cave dwellers and wolves?

   A The cave dwellers respected the wolves.

   B The cave dwellers feared the wolves.

   C The cave dwellers observed the wolves.

   D The cave dwellers imitated the wolves.

2. What does the word domesticated mean in this selection?

   A feared

   B faithful

   C friendly

   D tamed

3. What word means the opposite of scarce in this selection?

   A uncommon

   B plentiful

   C hidden

   D exposed

Read the selection below. Then, answer the questions. On your answer sheet, darken the circle for each correct answer.

For more than 80 years, Macy's, a large department store in New York City, has held a parade to <u>kick off</u> the start of the holiday season. People from all over the world come to see the <u>giant</u> balloons of their favorite TV and cartoon figures as the balloons move down the parade route. Some of the sculptures have included *Sesame Street* characters, Peter Rabbit, Bullwinkle, and Spiderman. Some of these balloon sculptures are as tall as a six-story building. Each figure has heavy ropes attached to it and is <u>anchored</u> with sandbags. The figures are led by a team of at least four people holding on to the ropes.

The night before the parade, many New Yorkers gather in Central Park to watch the balloons being inflated with helium. It takes a long time to fill the balloons, and workers usually work past midnight.

On the day of the parade, crowds of people <u>line</u> the route very early. The parade ends at the entrance to Macy's. Many people agree that this is a very special way to begin the season.

4. What does the expression <u>kick off</u> mean in this selection?

   A start

   B turn

   C hit with a foot

   D make someone leave

5. What does the word <u>anchored</u> mean in this selection?

   A lifted up

   B inflated

   C held down

   D filled with sand

6. Read this dictionary entry for the word <u>line</u>.

   > **line (līn)**
   > 1. *verb* to attach a cover to the inside of a garment such as a coat
   > 2. *verb* to mark with a line or lines
   > 3. *verb* to form a bordering line along something
   > 4. *verb* to place in a series or row

   Which definition matches how <u>line</u> is used in this selection?

   A Definition 1

   B Definition 2

   C Definition 3

   D Definition 4

Name _____ Date _____

On your answer sheet, darken the circle for each correct answer.

7. Choose the word that **best** completes the blank.

flower : garden = fish : _____ .

   A lawn

   B lake

   C tree

   D shark

8. Read these sentences. Choose the word that **best** completes **both** sentences.

The dogs would _____ for the woods when we went camping. The _____ of lightning struck a tree.

   A flash

   B bolt

   C run

   D race

9. Read the sentence.

I was exhausted after hiking up and down the steep canyon for hours, and my hiking boots felt like lead bricks.

   What is the meaning of the simile in this sentence?

   A The hiking boots were shaped like bricks.

   B The hiking boots were made of metal.

   C The hiking boots felt very hard.

   D The hiking boots felt very heavy.

On your answer sheet, darken the circle for each correct answer.

10. Read these sentences. Choose the word that **best** completes **both** sentences.

> We stripped the _____ from the tree.
>
> The two puppies _____ all night.

A limbs

B leaves

C run

D bark

11. Choose the word that **best** completes the sentence.

> The balloon _____ until it burst when Aaron blew too much air into it.

A deflated

B floated

C expanded

D popped

12. Choose the word that **best** completes the sentence.

> Petra's story of how the accident occurred was _____ because she included many facts and details.

A unbelievable

B believer

C disbelief

D believable

Writing Practice Test

Writing Prompt 1: Opinion

Plan, write, and proofread an opinion letter in response to the writing prompt below. Write the final draft of your letter on the next two pages.

What is your favorite activity? It might be a hobby, a sport, a game, or some other activity. Write an opinion letter to a children's magazine explaining why readers should try your favorite activity. Provide reasons that support your opinion, and include facts, details, and examples.

As you write your letter, be sure to

- Focus on the topic.

- Explain your opinion.

- Give reasons why students should try your activity and support it with details and examples.

- Organize your opinion letter so that your ideas have a logical order.

- Keep your audience in mind as you write.

- Edit your letter for correct grammar and usage.

Name _____ Date _____

Name _____ Date _____

_____

_____

_____

_____

_____

_____

_____

_____

_____

_____

_____

_____

_____

_____

_____

_____

_____

_____

_____

_____

_____

_____

_____

_____

_____

_____

_____

_____

_____

_____

Writing Prompt 2: Informative

Plan, write, and proofread an informative essay in response to the writing prompt below. Write the final draft of your essay on the next two pages.

> What qualities do you think are important in a friendship? Write an informative essay for children who are younger than you explaining how to be a good friend.

As you write your essay, be sure to

- Focus on the most important qualities of a good friend.
- Clearly state your main idea.
- Provide details and examples that support your main idea.
- Organize your writing and present your ideas in a logical order.
- Keep your audience in mind as you write.
- Edit your essay for correct grammar and usage.

_____

_____

_____

_____

_____

_____

_____

_____

_____

_____

_____

_____

_____

_____

_____

_____

_____

_____

_____

_____

_____

_____

_____

_____

_____

_____

_____

Name _____   Date _____

_____

_____

_____

_____

_____

_____

_____

_____

_____

_____

_____

_____

_____

_____

_____

_____

_____

_____

_____

_____

_____

_____

_____

_____

_____

_____

_____

_____

_____

_____

_____

_____

Writing Prompt 3: Narrative

Plan, write, and proofread a narrative story in response to the writing prompt below. Write the final draft of your story on the next two pages.

Write a story for a children's magazine about a time you achieved something through teamwork that you could not have done alone. You can write the story about a real experience or a made-up one. Describe in detail what you accomplished and how teamwork was necessary. Include characters and dialogue as you describe the events in the story.

As you write your essay, be sure to

- Focus on one accomplishment.

- Include sensory details about the events in your story.

- Explain why the event was significant.

- Organize your writing and present your ideas in a logical order.

- Develop your characters so readers understand them.

- Edit your essay for correct grammar and usage.

Name _____ Date _____

Name _____ Date _____

Answer Sheets

Reading Practice: Literature

1 Ⓐ Ⓑ Ⓒ Ⓓ
2 Ⓐ Ⓑ Ⓒ Ⓓ
3 Ⓐ Ⓑ Ⓒ Ⓓ
4 Ⓐ Ⓑ Ⓒ Ⓓ
5 Ⓐ Ⓑ Ⓒ Ⓓ
6 Ⓐ Ⓑ Ⓒ Ⓓ
7 Write answers on a separate sheet of paper.
8 Ⓐ Ⓑ Ⓒ Ⓓ
9 Ⓐ Ⓑ Ⓒ Ⓓ
10 Ⓐ Ⓑ Ⓒ Ⓓ
11 Ⓐ Ⓑ Ⓒ Ⓓ

12 Write answers on a separate sheet of paper.
13 Ⓐ Ⓑ Ⓒ Ⓓ
14 Ⓐ Ⓑ Ⓒ Ⓓ
15 Ⓐ Ⓑ Ⓒ Ⓓ
16 Ⓐ Ⓑ Ⓒ Ⓓ
17 Ⓐ Ⓑ Ⓒ Ⓓ
18 Ⓐ Ⓑ Ⓒ Ⓓ
19 Write answers on a separate sheet of paper.
20 Ⓐ Ⓑ Ⓒ Ⓓ
21 Ⓐ Ⓑ Ⓒ Ⓓ

22 Ⓐ Ⓑ Ⓒ Ⓓ
23 Ⓐ Ⓑ Ⓒ Ⓓ
24 Write answers on a separate sheet of paper.
25 Ⓐ Ⓑ Ⓒ Ⓓ
26 Ⓐ Ⓑ Ⓒ Ⓓ
27 Ⓐ Ⓑ Ⓒ Ⓓ
28 Ⓐ Ⓑ Ⓒ Ⓓ
29 Ⓐ Ⓑ Ⓒ Ⓓ
30 Write answers on a separate sheet of paper.

Reading Practice: Informational Text

1 Ⓐ Ⓑ Ⓒ Ⓓ
2 Ⓐ Ⓑ Ⓒ Ⓓ
3 Ⓐ Ⓑ Ⓒ Ⓓ
4 Ⓐ Ⓑ Ⓒ Ⓓ
5 Ⓐ Ⓑ Ⓒ Ⓓ
6 Ⓐ Ⓑ Ⓒ Ⓓ
7 Write answers on a separate sheet of paper.
8 Ⓐ Ⓑ Ⓒ Ⓓ
9 Ⓐ Ⓑ Ⓒ Ⓓ

10 Ⓐ Ⓑ Ⓒ Ⓓ
11 Ⓐ Ⓑ Ⓒ Ⓓ
12 Ⓐ Ⓑ Ⓒ Ⓓ
13 Ⓐ Ⓑ Ⓒ Ⓓ
14 Write answers on a separate sheet of paper.
15 Ⓐ Ⓑ Ⓒ Ⓓ
16 Ⓐ Ⓑ Ⓒ Ⓓ
17 Ⓐ Ⓑ Ⓒ Ⓓ
18 Ⓐ Ⓑ Ⓒ Ⓓ

19 Ⓐ Ⓑ Ⓒ Ⓓ
20 Write answers on a separate sheet of paper.
21 Ⓐ Ⓑ Ⓒ Ⓓ
22 Ⓐ Ⓑ Ⓒ Ⓓ
23 Ⓐ Ⓑ Ⓒ Ⓓ
24 Ⓐ Ⓑ Ⓒ Ⓓ
25 Ⓐ Ⓑ Ⓒ Ⓓ
26 Write answers on a separate sheet of paper.

Language Arts Practice

1 Write answers on a separate sheet of paper.
2 Ⓐ Ⓑ Ⓒ Ⓓ
3 Ⓐ Ⓑ Ⓒ Ⓓ
4 Ⓐ Ⓑ Ⓒ Ⓓ
5 Ⓐ Ⓑ Ⓒ Ⓓ
6 Ⓐ Ⓑ Ⓒ Ⓓ
7 Ⓐ Ⓑ Ⓒ Ⓓ
8 Ⓐ Ⓑ Ⓒ Ⓓ
9 Write answers on a separate sheet of paper.
10 Ⓐ Ⓑ Ⓒ Ⓓ
11 Ⓐ Ⓑ Ⓒ Ⓓ
12 Ⓐ Ⓑ Ⓒ Ⓓ
13 Ⓐ Ⓑ Ⓒ Ⓓ

14 Ⓐ Ⓑ Ⓒ Ⓓ
15 Ⓐ Ⓑ Ⓒ Ⓓ
16 Ⓐ Ⓑ Ⓒ Ⓓ
17 Ⓐ Ⓑ Ⓒ Ⓓ
18 Ⓐ Ⓑ Ⓒ Ⓓ
19 Ⓐ Ⓑ Ⓒ Ⓓ
20 Ⓐ Ⓑ Ⓒ Ⓓ
21 Ⓐ Ⓑ Ⓒ Ⓓ
22 Ⓐ Ⓑ Ⓒ Ⓓ
23 Ⓐ Ⓑ Ⓒ Ⓓ
24 Write answers on a separate sheet of paper.
25 Ⓐ Ⓑ Ⓒ Ⓓ
26 Write answers on a separate sheet of paper.

27 Ⓐ Ⓑ Ⓒ Ⓓ
28 Ⓐ Ⓑ Ⓒ Ⓓ
29 Ⓐ Ⓑ Ⓒ Ⓓ
30 Ⓐ Ⓑ Ⓒ Ⓓ
31 Ⓐ Ⓑ Ⓒ Ⓓ
32 Ⓐ Ⓑ Ⓒ Ⓓ
33 Ⓐ Ⓑ Ⓒ Ⓓ
34 Ⓐ Ⓑ Ⓒ Ⓓ
35 Ⓐ Ⓑ Ⓒ Ⓓ
36 Ⓐ Ⓑ Ⓒ Ⓓ
37 Ⓐ Ⓑ Ⓒ Ⓓ
38 Ⓐ Ⓑ Ⓒ Ⓓ
39 Ⓐ Ⓑ Ⓒ Ⓓ
40 Ⓐ Ⓑ Ⓒ Ⓓ

Vocabulary Practice

1 Ⓐ Ⓑ Ⓒ Ⓓ
2 Ⓐ Ⓑ Ⓒ Ⓓ
3 Ⓐ Ⓑ Ⓒ Ⓓ
4 Ⓐ Ⓑ Ⓒ Ⓓ
5 Ⓐ Ⓑ Ⓒ Ⓓ

6 Ⓐ Ⓑ Ⓒ Ⓓ
7 Ⓐ Ⓑ Ⓒ Ⓓ
8 Ⓐ Ⓑ Ⓒ Ⓓ
9 Ⓐ Ⓑ Ⓒ Ⓓ
10 Ⓐ Ⓑ Ⓒ Ⓓ

11 Ⓐ Ⓑ Ⓒ Ⓓ
12 Ⓐ Ⓑ Ⓒ Ⓓ
13 Ⓐ Ⓑ Ⓒ Ⓓ
14 Ⓐ Ⓑ Ⓒ Ⓓ
15 Ⓐ Ⓑ Ⓒ Ⓓ

Writing Practice

Write your final responses to the writing prompts on your own paper.

Reading Practice Test: Literature

1 Ⓐ Ⓑ Ⓒ Ⓓ
2 Ⓐ Ⓑ Ⓒ Ⓓ
3 Ⓐ Ⓑ Ⓒ Ⓓ
4 Ⓐ Ⓑ Ⓒ Ⓓ
5 Ⓐ Ⓑ Ⓒ Ⓓ
6 Ⓐ Ⓑ Ⓒ Ⓓ
7 Ⓐ Ⓑ Ⓒ Ⓓ
8 Ⓐ Ⓑ Ⓒ Ⓓ
9 Write answers on a separate sheet of paper.

10 Ⓐ Ⓑ Ⓒ Ⓓ
11 Ⓐ Ⓑ Ⓒ Ⓓ
12 Ⓐ Ⓑ Ⓒ Ⓓ
13 Ⓐ Ⓑ Ⓒ Ⓓ
14 Ⓐ Ⓑ Ⓒ Ⓓ
15 Ⓐ Ⓑ Ⓒ Ⓓ
16 Ⓐ Ⓑ Ⓒ Ⓓ
17 Write answers on a separate sheet of paper.
18 Ⓐ Ⓑ Ⓒ Ⓓ

19 Ⓐ Ⓑ Ⓒ Ⓓ
20 Ⓐ Ⓑ Ⓒ Ⓓ
21 Ⓐ Ⓑ Ⓒ Ⓓ
22 Ⓐ Ⓑ Ⓒ Ⓓ
23 Ⓐ Ⓑ Ⓒ Ⓓ
24 Ⓐ Ⓑ Ⓒ Ⓓ
25 Ⓐ Ⓑ Ⓒ Ⓓ
26 Write answers on a separate sheet of paper.

Reading Practice Test: Informational Text

1 Ⓐ Ⓑ Ⓒ Ⓓ
2 Ⓐ Ⓑ Ⓒ Ⓓ
3 Ⓐ Ⓑ Ⓒ Ⓓ
4 Ⓐ Ⓑ Ⓒ Ⓓ
5 Ⓐ Ⓑ Ⓒ Ⓓ
6 Ⓐ Ⓑ Ⓒ Ⓓ
7 Ⓐ Ⓑ Ⓒ Ⓓ

8 Ⓐ Ⓑ Ⓒ Ⓓ
9 Write answers on a separate sheet of paper.
10 Ⓐ Ⓑ Ⓒ Ⓓ
11 Ⓐ Ⓑ Ⓒ Ⓓ
12 Ⓐ Ⓑ Ⓒ Ⓓ
13 Ⓐ Ⓑ Ⓒ Ⓓ

14 Ⓐ Ⓑ Ⓒ Ⓓ
15 Ⓐ Ⓑ Ⓒ Ⓓ
16 Ⓐ Ⓑ Ⓒ Ⓓ
17 Ⓐ Ⓑ Ⓒ Ⓓ
18 Write answers on a separate sheet of paper.

Answer Sheets
Higher Scores on Reading and Language Arts, Grade 5

Language Arts Practice Test

1 Ⓐ Ⓑ Ⓒ Ⓓ
2 Write answers on a separate sheet of paper.
3 Ⓐ Ⓑ Ⓒ Ⓓ
4 Ⓐ Ⓑ Ⓒ Ⓓ
5 Ⓐ Ⓑ Ⓒ Ⓓ
6 Ⓐ Ⓑ Ⓒ Ⓓ
7 Ⓐ Ⓑ Ⓒ Ⓓ
8 Write answers on a separate sheet of paper.
9 Ⓐ Ⓑ Ⓒ Ⓓ
10 Ⓐ Ⓑ Ⓒ Ⓓ
11 Ⓐ Ⓑ Ⓒ Ⓓ
12 Ⓐ Ⓑ Ⓒ Ⓓ
13 Ⓐ Ⓑ Ⓒ Ⓓ

14 Ⓐ Ⓑ Ⓒ Ⓓ
15 Ⓐ Ⓑ Ⓒ Ⓓ
16 Ⓐ Ⓑ Ⓒ Ⓓ
17 Ⓐ Ⓑ Ⓒ Ⓓ
18 Ⓐ Ⓑ Ⓒ Ⓓ
19 Ⓐ Ⓑ Ⓒ Ⓓ
20 Ⓐ Ⓑ Ⓒ Ⓓ
21 Ⓐ Ⓑ Ⓒ Ⓓ
22 Write answers on a separate sheet of paper.
23 Ⓐ Ⓑ Ⓒ Ⓓ
24 Ⓐ Ⓑ Ⓒ Ⓓ
25 Ⓐ Ⓑ Ⓒ Ⓓ
26 Ⓐ Ⓑ Ⓒ Ⓓ

27 Write answers on a separate sheet of paper.
28 Ⓐ Ⓑ Ⓒ Ⓓ
29 Ⓐ Ⓑ Ⓒ Ⓓ
30 Ⓐ Ⓑ Ⓒ Ⓓ
31 Ⓐ Ⓑ Ⓒ Ⓓ
32 Ⓐ Ⓑ Ⓒ Ⓓ
33 Ⓐ Ⓑ Ⓒ Ⓓ
34 Ⓐ Ⓑ Ⓒ Ⓓ
35 Ⓐ Ⓑ Ⓒ Ⓓ
36 Ⓐ Ⓑ Ⓒ Ⓓ
37 Ⓐ Ⓑ Ⓒ Ⓓ
38 Ⓐ Ⓑ Ⓒ Ⓓ
39 Ⓐ Ⓑ Ⓒ Ⓓ

Vocabulary Practice Test

1 Ⓐ Ⓑ Ⓒ Ⓓ
2 Ⓐ Ⓑ Ⓒ Ⓓ
3 Ⓐ Ⓑ Ⓒ Ⓓ
4 Ⓐ Ⓑ Ⓒ Ⓓ

5 Ⓐ Ⓑ Ⓒ Ⓓ
6 Ⓐ Ⓑ Ⓒ Ⓓ
7 Ⓐ Ⓑ Ⓒ Ⓓ
8 Ⓐ Ⓑ Ⓒ Ⓓ

9 Ⓐ Ⓑ Ⓒ Ⓓ
10 Ⓐ Ⓑ Ⓒ Ⓓ
11 Ⓐ Ⓑ Ⓒ Ⓓ
12 Ⓐ Ⓑ Ⓒ Ⓓ

Writing Practice

Write your final responses to the writing prompts in the space provided.

Answer Key

Reading Practice: Literature

1. C
2. D
3. A
4. B
5. A
6. C
7. When a hungry traveler arrives in a village, the selfish villagers don't want to share their food. The traveler puts stones and water in a pot to make soup and then tricks people into donating ingredients. The traveler shares his soup with the villagers, who don't realize the trick.
8. B
9. A
10. B
11. D
12. The science fair didn't go as planned because the display fell over and Rick's worm house fell on the floor.
13. C
14. D
15. A
16. C
17. B
18. D
19. Andrew tells the girl and her father that they found the missing kitten, but Jon hesitates and feels sad about returning the kitten.
20. C
21. A
22. C
23. B
24. Possible response: The lines create a mood of excitement as the speaker captures just a glimpse of the fish. The fish appeals to the sense of sight with words like *silver* and *glistening*. These words also help you picture how the fish is something valuable or desirable.

25. D
26. D
27. A
28. B
29. B
30. Possible response: The poem appeals to the reader's sense of sight by describing how colors appear to weave together in the sky. It appeals to sound by comparing the rainstorm to an orchestra. It also compares the rain to a shower that gently cleans the ground. It appeals to the sense of taste by mentioning the sweet drops of rain.

Reading Practice: Informational Text

1. C
2. A
3. C
4. A
5. D
6. B
7. Possible response: Halley's Comet is named after Edmund Halley, who used scientific theories to predict the comet's appearance every 76 years.
8. D
9. C
10. B
11. B
12. A
13. D
14. Possible response: George Washington had several important roles in forming and leading the United States. He led troops, helped create the Constitution, was elected the country's first president, and guided the country through challenging situations.
15. C
16. A
17. C
18. D

19. B

20. Possible response: The author probably lists the materials first so that a person has everything needed to complete the project before starting.

21. A

22. B

23. D

24. C

25. B

26. Possible response: This selection explains how to do a trick using common objects. Paper clips and a rubber band are placed on a strip of paper. When the ends of the paper are pulled, the paper clips and rubber band are "magically" linked together.

Language Arts Practice

1. A box turtle is a reptile that lives in woods and fields.

2. B

3. D

4. A

5. C

6. B

7. C

8. C

9. You stand on the board sideways and face the direction you want to go.

10. D

11. B

12. D

13. A

14. B

15. A

16. C

17. A

18. A

19. D

20. B

21. C

22. B

23. A

24. When people wanted to describe something very large, they said it was jumbo size.

25. C

26. Jove, a Greek god, had many sons.

27. D

28. C

29. A

30. A

31. B

32. A

33. D

34. D

35. B

36. C

37. A

38. C

39. A

40. D

Vocabulary Practice

1. D

2. A

3. B

4. D

5. C

6. C

7. A

8. B

9. D

10. B

11. A

12. D

13. B

14. C

15. C

Writing Practice

See the scoring rubrics on pages 56–58.

Reading Practice Test: Literature

1. D
2. C
3. B
4. A
5. C
6. D
7. B
8. C
9. Possible response: Russ is looking forward to the journey because it has been his dream. Kathryn, on the other hand, is sullen and unhappy about leaving her friends and the family's comfortable home.
10. A
11. B
12. D
13. C
14. A
15. B
16. C
17. Possible response: Ravi's parents work as a team and respect each other's opinions. For example, they listen to each other's views and both agree that Ravi can take care of Rufus. They are also strict but understanding. Mr. Nellore speaks sternly to his son, but he listens to Ravi and allows him to care for the dog.
18. D
19. D
20. C
21. B
22. C
23. A
24. B
25. C
26. Possible response: The speaker admires the ants because they are hardworking. He compares them to an army of bulldozers and construction workers. He also mentions that they do their work quickly and don't complain about it.

Reading Practice Test: Informational Text

1. C
2. B
3. C
4. A
5. A
6. B
7. D
8. B
9. Possible response: Mary Bethune helped African American women get the right to vote. In addition, she helped educate African American girls by starting her own school.
10. D
11. D
12. C
13. C
14. B
15. D
16. A
17. A
18. Possible response: The scale needs to be completely covered with tape or the markings could be washed off. In addition, if it is not placed in the correct direction, it might not give an accurate reading.

Language Arts Practice Test

1. B
2. Beside the wagons, armed men walked cautiously.
3. C
4. D
5. A
6. A
7. C
8. You'll need comfortable shoes or boots.
9. C
10. D
11. D
12. B

13. C

14. A

15. B

16. C

17. C

18. B

19. D

20. A

21. D

22. It was followed by an unusual, squeaky car horn.

23. C

24. C

25. A

26. C

27. "Here, sample this," he might say.

28. A

29. B

30. C

31. D

32. B

33. A

34. D

35. A

36. B

37. C

38. D

39. A

Vocabulary Practice Test

1. A

2. D

3. B

4. A

5. C

6. C

7. B

8. B

9. D

10. D

11. C

12. D

Writing Practice Test

See the scoring rubrics on pages 56–58.